*This book is dedicated to
the loving memory of Vo Rogue,
our once in a lifetime champion, who took us
on the ride of a lifetime and made
a nation of racing followers so very happy.*

Published by Melbourne Books
Level 9, 100 Collins Street,
Melbourne, VIC 3000
Australia
www.melbournebooks.com.au
info@melbournebooks.com.au

Copyright © Lynlea Small 2022

All rights reserved. No part of this publication may be reproduced, stored in a retrieval system, or transmitted in any form or any means electronic, mechanical, photocopying, recording or otherwise without the prior permission of the publisher.

Title: The Vo Rogue Show
Author: Lynlea Small
ISBN: 9781877096396

 A catalogue record for this book is available from the National Library of Australia

Front cover image: Vo Rogue going to the barriers for the Group 1 MacKinnon Stakes. Flemington 4 November 1989. *Photo: Steve Hart Photographics*

Back cover image: Team Vo after winning 1988 St George Stakes. Caulfield 27 February 1988. *Photo: Martin King/Sportspix*

Page 1: Vo Rogue after winning the Qantas Brisbane Handicap in November 1988. Vo was often described by the press as plain. I never saw anything plain in this horse. To me, he always portrayed beauty and intelligence. *Photo: Noel Pascoe*

THE
VO ROGUE SHOW

Lynlea Small

M
MELBOURNE BOOKS

CONTENTS

FOREWORD		7
INTRODUCTON		11
PART I	THE STORY BEGINS	
Chapter 1	That Can't Be The Horse I Bought … Erk	17
Chapter 2	Cyril	26
Chapter 3	From Erky To Athlete	32
Chapter 4	First Trip To Melbourne	38
Chapter 5	The Spring Of '87	49
Chapter 6	A Legend Is Born	54
Chapter 7	The Match Race Of The Century	64
Chapter 8	The Spring Of '88	79
Chapter 9	The Autumn Of '89	90
Chapter 10	The Spring Of '89	97
Chapter 11	The Autumn Of '90	110
Chapter 12	The Beginning Of The End	122
Chapter 13	Statistics Of Interest	128
PART II	THE STORY CONTINUES FOR SOME	
Chapter 14	Living Life Post-Vo Rogue	139
Chapter 15	The Hendra Virus Claims Vic's Life	147
Chapter 16	Cyril's Bad Fall	158
Chapter 17	Vo's Final Years	164
Chapter 18	Carrying On The Tradition	169
Chapter 19	Overcoming Adversity	176
Chapter 20	Much To Celebrate	186
ACKNOWLEDGEMENTS		196
THE AUTHOR		199

FOREWORD

From first light on Sunday March 29 2009, you could tell South East Queensland was in for another day of high temperatures and oppressive humidity. Conditions had been stifling at the Parklands Paceway the previous evening when American import Mr Feelgood thwarted Blacks A Fake's quest for four consecutive Interdominion Grand Finals.

The humidity was punishing when I arrived at Cyril and Lynlea Small's Tallebudgera Valley property with a Sky Channel camera crew the following morning. I didn't want to spend time on the Gold Coast without paying a visit to long-retired champion Vo Rogue who was spending time with the Smalls as he battled with a chronic bout of laminitis. He'd spent most of his time following retirement in the care of part-owner Jeff Perry, who owned a property just four kilometres away. The sensitive nature of the laminitis made it difficult for the 25-year-old gelding to move about on the undulating terrain of the Perry farm. He was clearly more comfortable on the flatter acreage of the Small property.

The camera crew had barely rolled tape when the unthinkable happened. The old horse toppled to the ground as Cyril Small led him from the paddock. The champion's former jockey reacted quickly. He grabbed a nearby hose and sprayed water over Vo's prostrate form from nose to tail. The result was astounding. Vo Rogue clambered to his feet after a couple of minutes, looking none the worse for wear. Cyril's diagnosis was correct. The grand old horse was a victim of heat exhaustion.

We couldn't wait to get into the house and to the blissful relief of air conditioning where interviews with Jeff Perry and Cyril could be recorded. The audio operator delivered the grim news that the aircon motor was too loud and would have to be switched off. It was still as hot as it gets, but a big improvement on the outdoor location. We got the interviews underway.

Jeff and John Murray had jointly purchased Vo Rogue as a weanling and raced the horse in partnership until early 1988, when John decided to put his 20 per cent share on the market. That share was purchased by Victorian Garry Roberts whose timing couldn't have been more fortuitous. The horse had won a Group 1 and four Group 2 races to that point, but his glory days were all ahead of him. Jeff Perry's devotion to his once in a lifetime horse extended far beyond the racetrack and endured until the champion took his final breath in 2012.

Almost as clear in my mind as that sultry morning at Tallebudgera Valley is the visit I paid with a Channel 9 News crew to the stabling complex at the back of Kembla Grange racecourse in the spring of 1989. Vo Rogue was stabled there for a short Sydney campaign. To this point in time, the gelding hadn't won in the harbour city, and some detractors were doubting that he ever would. This was the first time I'd been close enough to lay a hand on the popular horse. It was also my first encounter with his trainer Vic Rail, whose unorthodox methods had garnered almost as much publicity as Vo Rogue's spectacular front running wins.

I got the shock of my life when the nuggety former jockey greeted us in the stable breezeway. Vic was garbed in a T-shirt, stubby shorts and thongs. He was obviously oblivious to the golden rule that you never wear thongs around horses. I couldn't help but think of Tommy Smith and Bart Cummings who usually wore a jacket and tie whenever media people visited the stables. I wondered if Vic would do anything to substantiate the popular opinion that he was a tad eccentric. The Queensland horseman duly obliged.

'This is the quietest thoroughbred you'll ever see,' said the Queensland horseman. 'Watch this and I'll show you what I mean.'

The Channel 9 cameraman captured a priceless piece of footage as Vic handed the lead rope to an assistant and proceeded to do something that most horsemen would never risk. He stooped low and slid between the horse's front legs before continuing on with his head brushing Vo's belly. He calmly exited between the horse's hind legs with a huge smile on his face. That remarkable gelding didn't blink throughout the well-rehearsed procedure.

I thought of that special morning at Kembla Grange when the sad news filtered through from Brisbane five years later that Vic Rail had died after becoming infected with Hendra virus.

Nobody can tell you why this unique racehorse failed to strike his best form in eight Sydney runs, recording just one win and finishing unplaced in the other seven. I'm glad I was there to call his all the way win in the 1989 Group 1 George Main Stakes. He looked vulnerable when Groucho and Don't Play threatened danger in the straight, but it was almost as though he knew his reputation depended on that Group 1 win. Cyril got him home, the crowd loved it and the Randwick fans forgave his previous failures in Sydney.

The Cyril Small factor added greatly to the romance of the Vo Rogue story. The hard-working Brisbane jockey partnered the amazing horse in 22 of his 26 wins. It's a pity that he's credited with only six Group 1 wins on the gelding. Under today's rankings, Vo's three Orr Stakes wins and two Turnbull Stakes victories would be classified as Group 1s.

Vo Rogue exited the racetrack in 1991. Cyril Small is still going at age 63. His opportunities are infrequent these days, but Lynlea says he's as keen as a fledgling apprentice when offered a race ride. The veteran rode his first winner in May of 1974 and has less than two years to go before he realises a burning ambition to complete 50 years as a professional jockey. Is it any wonder Cyril Small and Vo Rogue got on so well?

Cyril and Lynlea are the proud parents of Daniel (33), Braidon (31) and Jessica (28). Braidon is already an accomplished jumps jockey in Victoria, while Daniel made his debut in the same business on 18 April 2022 in a steeplechase event. Just 25 days later, on 13 May and at his fourth ride, Daniel rode his first winner Ferago in a highweight race at Geelong.

Lynlea has made her mark as a trainer, posting notable success with a handful of horses. How she handles her whirlwind lifestyle is a source of wonderment to family and friends. In 2019 she was confirmed with her Doctor of Philosophy after completing a three-year course while working full-time at a local university.

This book has been high on Lynlea's list of priorities for several years now. In her trademark style this dynamo has painstakingly researched press clippings, viewed race replays until her head spun and sought anecdotes from those whose lives were touched by Vo Rogue. The result is a touching, sensitive and beautifully written account of one of the greatest racehorses of his generation.

Incidentally, a few years ago a friend gave me a framed photograph of a modest monument standing just inside the boundary fence of a property near Timaru on New Zealand's South Island. The monument marks the spot where Phar Lap was foaled in 1926. After that, I did a double take when, for the first time, I spotted an expertly painted sign at the front gate of a Pitt Town property on the outskirts of Sydney. The inscription was brief. It said 'The birthplace of Vo Rogue'. How fitting it was that the 1980s super horse should be afforded a similar honour.

John Tapp OAM

INTRODUCTON

Vo Rogue is without doubt one of Australia's most beloved racehorses. In the late 1980s and early 1990s, Vo Rogue was the people's champion and star of The Vo Rogue Show that played to packed grandstands on Australia's best racecourses for five years. Vic Rail, Cyril Small, Jeff Perry and, to a lesser degree, Garry Roberts were the support acts.

It has been over 30 years since Vo Rogue—or Vo to his family, friends and fans—last raced and a decade has passed since he crossed over the rainbow bridge. Absence makes the heart grow fonder and for the old and new fans of Vo that expression stands true. The horse is loved as much today as he ever was. His racecourse feats are replayed over and over again on Racing.com, much to the delight of his legion of fans. Each year in March he is remembered for his sterling wins in two Australian Cups and his courageous seconds in the same race. 'Doing a Vo Rogue' has become a catchcry for race callers across Australia when horses go out with big leads in races.

But Vo was more than a racehorse; he was family to those that cared for him and loved him.

People think they know Vo's story and that of the people who were instrumental in bringing 'The Vo Rogue Show' to life. No doubt they know some of it, bits and pieces accompanied by what they read in the press, hear on the television or hear from a mate, none of which are always reliable. I thought it was time that racing fans and the general public were given a factual account of what is, in reality, many stories.

This book tells the story from beginning to end, commencing with how Jeff Perry, Vic Rail, Cyril Small and later Garry Roberts, found themselves teaming up with a horse who in simple terms made people happy and took them all on the ride of a lifetime. The story details how a small, gelded weanling of poor breeding initially called 'Erky' and purchased with the proceeds of a punt, blossomed into a superstar racehorse. This is a love story between the horse and his senior part-owner Jeff Perry. It is also a story of the solidarity of one man for his mates whose individual talents he respected and trusted despite some tumultuous moments in their relationships.

For some, the story has continued well after Vo retired and so this book moves beyond Vo's racing days and follows the lives of his connections and their trials and tribulations as they navigate life without their superstar galloper by their sides.

This book is not just a story about horse racing. It is a story about life, death, resilience, the undying love for a horse, and the story of a friendship between two men that has lasted for close to forty years.

My name is Lynlea Small. I am the wife of Vo's regular jockey Cyril and a long-time friend to Vo's senior part-owner Jeff Perry and his beautiful daughter Cymone. I recount this story to you through my own lens and that of those most closely connected to Vo, with the support of racing statistics sourced from Racing Australia and other racing networks. Additionally, the book refers to countless newspaper articles I gathered and have kept for more than 35 years to take you back in time so you can either reminisce or, if you weren't there, you may gain an appreciation for that era of horse racing and what occurred during Vo's time on centre stage.

As the saying goes, they came, they saw, they conquered. But they did more than that. This story is what I know to be true.

So make yourself a cuppa, pour a glass of wine, or grab a beer, and settle in to your favourite chair with your feet up as I tell you the story of a once in a lifetime racehorse who captivated the nation, created a cult following and enriched the lives of those who knew and loved him.

The Vo Rogue Show ... is by Runyon from Cinderella.

— **Les Carlyon**
The Age 13 March 1989

PART I

THE STORY BEGINS

CHAPTER 1

THAT CAN'T BE THE HORSE I BOUGHT ... ERK

On 12 November 1983, a plain brown thoroughbred colt made his way into the world in a paddock near Windsor northwest of Sydney. Neither his mother Vow nor his father Ivor Prince were successful on the racetrack, and he too appeared nondescript. When he was seven months old, his breeder Dr Lance Merchant moved him, his mother and two fillies to a cattle property near Yass called Wylandra. The property was owned by Colin Grant.

In later years, journalist Heather Brown interviewed Mr Grant for a story that was published in *The Australian* magazine in August 1989. Mr Grant explained that it was his opinion that Dr Merchant was losing interest in breeding horses, and Dr Merchant told him to, 'Take them, look after them and take your pick of the young ones.'

Mr Grant selected the young colt that he later gelded and he told Ms Brown that the young horse was slow to come out of the anaesthetic after his gelding operation. 'It's funny, but the vet looked at me and said, "Well, you can see that one's no good, he hasn't any heart."'

Meanwhile, as the weanling recovered from his gelding operation, his half-brother Rode Rouge, by the stallion Devorant, was showing a great deal of promise on the track. Rode Rouge was foaled on 2 November 1982 and the colt was one year older than the weanling. Rode Rouge was being trained at a stable in Hendra in the northern suburbs of Brisbane by an interesting fellow by the name of Victory Robert Rail, Vic or Vicky to his friends. Vic was born in Townsville on 15 August 1945, the day that Japan surrendered and World War II came to an end, hence, his parents William and Doris named him Victory.

Rode Rouge was owned by a syndicate that was managed by John Murray, a car salesman from the Sunshine Coast. Initially, trainer Bill Wehlow of Gunsynd fame was approached to train the horse along with a filly called Lassiter's Ghost, however the Wehlow stable was full. Vic had pivoted between being a jockey, strapper, trackwork rider, foreman, farrier and trainer for 20 years and at that time had not long regained his trainer's licence. While he built up his clientele, Vic worked part-time for the Wehlow stable. Mr Wehlow recommended to Mr Murray that he give both the colt and the filly to Vic to train.

With Rode Rouge showing much promise on the track, Mr Murray became aware that he had a half-brother and contacted the breeder Dr Merchant. In the interview with Heather Brown, Colin Grant told her that Mr Murray offered Dr Merchant $1500 for the Ivor Prince weanling. Mr Grant claimed that he told Dr Merchant that the weanling was worth more, definitely $2500.

Mr Murray approached Vic's long-time client and close friend Jeff Perry to buy the gelded weanling with him, to which Jeff agreed. Jeff took an 80 per cent share and paid Mr Murray $4000 for it. Mr Murray kept the other 20 per cent share. Many weeks later, at the age of 11 months old, the nondescript weanling found himself on a horse float headed to Hendra and into the care of his new senior part-owner Jeff Perry and his trainer Vic Rail.

* * *

Jeff Perry is a no-nonsense man with a quick wit, well-known for his one-liners. His teaming up with Vic Rail seemed unlikely from a young age because as a child Jeff had no real interest in horses. The only contact Jeff had with them was with the draft horses used to cultivate the paddocks on the family farm at Aspley. Born to parents George and Elma in Nambour on 26 July 1950, the family, including his older sister Lynette, moved to the northern suburb of Brisbane when Jeff was three years old.

George enjoyed going to the races, but it wasn't until Jeff was 16 or 17 that he would commence sharing his father's passion for horse racing. Jeff had a mate who was doing some strapping work for a trainer in Hendra and Jeff would drop in to see him. Jeff recalls, 'One thing sort of led to another and next thing it's, "oh hold this horse and give it a pick" sort of thing, and my interest in horses and racing grew from there.'

In the early 1970s Jeff started doing some casual work for local equine veterinarian Dr Henry Hengge who was also training racehorses. Dr Hengge had a horse that no one could ride and Jeff remembers it as one of the maddest horses he has ever worked with. 'It would try and kill you, it was a bastard,' recalls Jeff. 'No one could ride it.'

No one, except for Vic Rail—who at the time had just returned from Melbourne and had started riding trackwork. 'Vic jumped on the horse and rode it in all its work,' says Jeff.

With Jeff strapping for Dr Hengge and Vic riding trackwork, the two soon became friends. Vic took out a trainer's licence and the two mates set about identifying and buying cheap horses that showed potential. Their first horse was Miss Winfred. 'She won five or six races,' says Jeff. 'Then we had some others and then we got a team of slow ones. And when I say slow, I mean *slow*. We were taking them to Kumbia and those sort of places, Mount Perry, Eidsvold, Wondai and couldn't do any good with them. They were hard days. You might as well say we went arse-over with the horses, we weren't doing any good. So I went back working.'

Jeff's work was in the earthmoving industry; drag lines, digging gravel and earthmoving. Jeff owned four drag lines at that time and placed them out for hire. 'We started at the Brisbane airport in 1979 and we worked there until 1984,' Jeff explained. 'We worked there continuously, plus a few other places too. We used to work long hours—12-hour days, six days a week, and on the seventh day we repaired the machines so we could start again on the Monday. So really, we were working seven days a week. We were down where the Brisbane airport is now when all there was were snakes, blow flies and mozzies. The first runway was built on swamp. Our first job was to drain the swamp. Then we did the bung walls for the first runway.'

* * *

While Jeff's love for racehorses was sparked as a teenager, Vic was destined for a life in the racing industry. As the seventh of nine children (one sibling sadly passed away as a toddler), Vic would prove that he was as good a horseman as most and he wanted nothing more than to be a jockey, just like his older brother Billy. At the age of 15, he became apprenticed to Townsville trainer Arthur 'Sadie' Standley. Vic was quite the athlete and he also took up amateur boxing and won three junior North Queensland Golden Gloves boxing championships.

In 1963 Vic made the decision to move south and had his apprenticeship transferred to trainer Jim Griffiths who at the time was training in Brisbane. The minimum riding weight was 7st 4lb (46.5kg), but within 18 months weight got the better of Vic. Not one who was easily deterred, Vic took off to Melbourne and had a crack over the jumps where the weight scale was, and still is, higher than flat races. At that time, it was 9st (57kg). That vocation was short-lived and unsuccessful.

Funnily enough, Cyril and I met former jumps jockey, now trainer, Kelvin Bourke some 25 years ago when he was in Brisbane for the Winter Racing Carnival. He told us the story of riding in a jumps race against Vic. Kelvin fell from the horse he was riding, and at the time he fell, the horse Vic was riding was about 200 metres behind him. Sure enough, Kelvin told us, Vic and his horse ran straight over the top of Kelvin who was still lying on the ground.

In the mid-1960s Vic worked as a strapper and trackwork rider and also learned the craft of a farrier as he moved back and forth between Brisbane and Melbourne. However, the turning point for Vic —that would be realised much later—came in the late 1960s when he became stable foreman for trainer Tommy Woodcock, forever famous and much-loved for being the strapper of the champion of all champions, the immortal Phar Lap, and the trainer of Reckless. It was those five years with Tommy that Vic would gain the knowledge and experience needed to one day train a champion of his own.

Vic was never one to let the grass grow under his feet. Having gone 'arse-over' with the horses, and his number one client off building the airport runway and earning a quid or several, Vic's desire to return to the saddle got the better of him. He threw in his trainer's licence and in late 1981, he did an extraordinary job to lose significant weight, which allowed him to take out a jockey's licence once again. Vic created a low-calorie diet that was not for everyone, and most definitely not for me. For a whole month, excluding Saturdays, Vic ate only cabbage, tomato and a small amount of liver and egg whites each day. He had half a lemon every morning and sucked on staminade ice blocks throughout the day. He allowed himself a reprieve each Saturday and ate whatever he wanted, only to recommence his rigid diet on the Sunday. When Vic started his diet he weighed 73kg, four weeks later, he weighed 50kg, losing a remarkable 23kg. In late November 1981, Vic had his first race ride after almost 18 years at Eidsvoid, 430km north of Brisbane.

* * *

At about the same time, Vic met a new trackwork rider, Debby Osborne. Debby was 19 and Vic was 36. They soon became inseparable. By then, Vic was divorced from his former wife Colleen with whom he had two sons, Chris and Troy.

Vic taught Debby how to be a top-notch trackwork rider and horse person and once she had honed her skills, Vic encouraged Debby to apply for her jockey's licence. Debby had to apply multiple times before she was finally successful in 1983. Debby explains that, 'When I first applied, I was told I was too old. I was then told that girls can only become apprenticed if they were related to their master, like a father–daughter scenario. I applied again and was told I was too tall, and then I was too heavy, but every time they put me on the scales I weighed 50 to 51kg. I just kept applying and they ran out of excuses. I was initially granted a licence to ride in the country and then later my licence was upgraded to ride on the provincial tracks. I didn't have to do an apprenticeship, but I think I was the last female to be granted a jockey's licence without doing an apprenticeship. After that, they started apprenticing girls.'

Haven't we come a long way in the past 40-odd years? I think we have, and for that we can thank a very determined, resilient and much-celebrated national treasure Pam O'Neill OAM, whose tireless efforts as a pioneering female jockey back in the late '70s cleared the way for other women to follow. Female jockeys now dominate country and provincial meetings across Australia, and they have a firm foothold among the metropolitan riding ranks. Jamie Kah not only became the first female to win the Victorian metropolitan premiership in 2021, she set an all-time record for the most wins in a season by any jockey, and took out the prestigious Scobie Breasley Medal. And of course, in 2015 Michelle Payne OAM became the first, and to date the only female, to win the Melbourne Cup. Who will ever forget Michelle telling everyone who thought women weren't strong enough to 'get stuffed'? Pure gold!

Today, female jockeys are not discriminated against on the basis of age, gender, parentage, height and to some degree, weight—although obviously the vocation of being a jockey *does* require that the licence-holder is able to ride within certain weight limits. Interestingly though, we still read the name Ms Jamie Kah or Ms Michelle Payne. We don't read the name Mr Hugh Bowman or Mr James McDonald. Why do you think that is? I don't know the answer myself, but I assume it has something to do with keeping the public informed as to whether the horse is being ridden by a man or a woman. But I digress.

Vic's comeback in the saddle lasted less than two years and he returned to training, renting stables in Harding Street in Hendra. He started with one horse called Wobbley, a son of Miss Winifred and from there, Vic slowly built up his clientele.

'Vic was also a very good spray painter and panelbeater', Debby tells me. 'He used to turn old VWs into convertibles.' To subsidise his income while he was building up his stable, as well as working part-time for Bill Wehlow, Vic also worked at Humes Body Shop in Albion, just north of the Brisbane CBD. That business specialised in prestige cars. Debby would often help out.

* * *

Although he worked long hours, Jeff retained his interest in racing, and with Vic re-establishing his training career, Jeff visited Vic's stables three or four afternoons a week on his way home from work. Jeff explained that, 'After the airport job finished in 1984, I'd had enough. I gave working away for a while and leased out my machines to other operators.' By that time, Vic was training close to a dozen horses for a number of other clients.

Jeff bought a horse called Lord Norm from trainer Fred Thomas that Vic trained for him. The horse won seven or eight races on provincial and country tracks. Jeff was never shy of a punt and won a nice sum of money with Lord Norm. Of his trainer, Jeff has this to say: 'Vic knew how to train a horse. There's no doubt about that. And I wouldn't say he's the best judge I've seen but he was a very good judge; he could tell you "This horse needs another gallop" or "He's right, ready to win". And he was a very good work rider, Vic—there's no doubt about it.'

Vic's judgement about Lord Norm's readiness to win a particular race in country South East Queensland would be the catalyst for one of the greatest stories to unfold in Australian racing history, because it was with those winnings that Jeff bought the 80 per cent share in the gelded weanling, sight unseen.

* * *

The gelded weanling arrived at Vic's stables one Saturday night in October 1984. The next morning, Jeff walked into the stables as he did most Sundays. He saw the small young horse in the sand roll. 'What's that horse in the sand roll Victor?' Jeff asked.

'Well, that's gotta be your horse because that's the only one coming up that I know of,' replied Vic.

'Geez,' Jeff said, 'that's not him, that can't be the horse that I've bought.'

Jeff recalls that the horse looked like a big Great Dane dog. He certainly didn't look like the horse he thought he had purchased. Jeff had been told that the young horse he bought looked just like Rode Rouge, only he was bay. Rode Rouge was a stunning looking individual, a chestnut with a white blaze and long white socks on both hind legs, with a short white sock on his near side front. While the weanling's registration papers listed him as bay in colour, he was actually a brown horse, and had no obvious white markings.

The weanling was not just small but also in very poor condition. The only word Jeff could find to describe his looks was '*Erk!*' Vic agreed that 'Erky' was weedy and looked like the runt of the litter but reminded Jeff that the horse was only a baby, he would grow, and maybe they might get to like him.

Jeff explains that the initial plan was to ready the horse for the yearling sales, but on seeing him that plan was aborted. The horse was in such a poor state that Jeff wanted to send him back to Yass but Vic was concerned that the young horse would not fare well on a return float trip and that he may well die. It would be necessary to feed the horse up prior to travelling him anywhere.

Debby Osborne well remembers the little horse arriving at the stables. She too agrees that Erky looked like a Great Dane dog and he was small and weak. Debby adds, 'He was a sensible little fellow.'

Debby recalls the day that Jeff was cleaning out the straw from the young horse's feet. The stable door was open and so was the gate leading out from the stable complex. All of a sudden Erky took off. Debby, who has always referred to Jeff by his nickname 'Froggy', says, 'Froggy grabbed his tail and skied up the barn behind the horse leaving rubber marks on the concrete. Erky never kicked out, he just stopped.'

After six weeks, Jeff got to know the young horse well and gained an appreciation for his intelligence. Jeff more than got to like him.

In Jeff's words, 'I fell in love with him.'

CHAPTER 2

CYRIL

With six weeks of stabling, good feed and lots of care behind him, Erky was strong enough to be sent to a paddock to grow. The paddock was on Bobby Gill's property, a former dairy farm on Nudgee Road at Northgate in the northern suburbs of Brisbane, not far from Hendra. In preparation for Erky's spell, and throughout his life when spelling, Jeff and Vic mixed sump oil with kerosene and rubbed it under his mane, along his back and down to his tail to protect the horse's skin from rain scald.

With Erky in the paddock, attention had turned to his two-year-old half-brother Rode Rouge. The colt was proving troublesome for Vic at the barriers. Although he had several jockeys riding for him, there was one young jockey in particular Vic sought out to help him resolve this problem. That jockey was Cyril Small. While he was quiet and unassuming, Cyril had built himself a reputation among the local racing fraternity as a master horseman, excellent educator of young horses, a good money rider and a trusted and reliable jockey with a tireless work ethic.

* * *

Originally from Casino in the Northern Rivers of New South Wales, Cyril James Small was riding horses before he could walk. Born to parents Bob and Eunice on 7 February 1959, Cyril was the fifth of six children, with twins Mervyn and Pauline being the oldest, then Barbara, Keith, Cyril and 14 months later Warren came along. Bob was an amateur jockey, horse trainer, breeder and punter who owned and operated a grazing property of mostly Hereford. Cyril was always an eager helper on the farm. Sadly, Eunice passed away from illness only six days after Cyril's eleventh birthday.

From the age of 12, Cyril rode competitively at the bridle meetings. Then at the age of 15 and in year nine at Marist Brothers College in Casino, he became apprenticed as a jockey to Casino trainer Stan Rayner and moved into Mr Rayner's family home. Back then, apprentices lived with the trainer they were apprenticed to who were called their masters.

Cyril's day began with pre-dawn trackwork riding up to 10 horses each morning, followed by stable chores, breakfast then school. After school he would have a quick snack before he would head back to the stables, then he would go home for dinner, homework and bed. The next morning he would get up and do it all over again.

Cyril had his first race ride at Casino on 4 May 1974 on a horse called Santow Mac. He guided the horse into fifth place and earned $15 for his trouble. Back in those days on the Northern Rivers, there was no such thing as jockey managers, with acceptances released and jockeys declared days before the race meeting. On the contrary. Jockeys were declared one hour prior to the first race. Cyril would turn up to the meeting, saddle and gear in hand and hope to secure a ride. There were five races per meeting and one meeting per week.

Cyril waited three weeks for his next ride, again at Casino and the tiny blond-haired blue-eyed 15-year-old was successful on Wunderbar in a Flying Welter over 1000 metres for local trainer Brian Allen. That would be his only winner in the 1973/74 racing season. Racing seasons run from 1 August to 31 July.

The next season (1974/75) while still at school, Cyril rode 29 winners. At the end of 1975 and having completed Year 10, Cyril left school to concentrate fully on his apprenticeship, and concentrate he did. In his second full season of race riding (1975/76) and just 17 years old, Cyril won both the apprentice and senior jockeys' premierships on the Northern Rivers with 55 wins, and in doing so set a race riding record that would stand for 25 years. A young star apprentice called Zac Purton broke the record in the 2000/01 racing season with 63 wins, a record that stands today. Zac is now a world-class jockey based in Hong Kong.

In that same 1975/76 racing season, star apprentice Malcolm Johnston who earned the nickname 'Miracle', also won the apprentices' and the senior jockeys' premierships in Sydney with a record 107.5 wins. His dominance resulted in the Australian Jockey Club changing the rules of racing for all apprentices. Racing Victoria's website explains that the rules that existed at that time 'permitted apprentices to claim an allowance of 1.5kg until they completed their indentures.' The new rule saw apprentices lose their claim when they had ridden 60 winners.

Cyril had ridden 85 winners across the Northern Rivers by that time, so he was left without a claim in that area which was deemed a country racing region. He still had just under four years left of his apprenticeship to serve because back in those days, apprentices did not become senior riders until they turned twenty-one. It was a tough time for a young apprentice riding against the senior jockeys on equal terms and even more so because the wins in the Northern Rivers were also counted toward any wins in provincial areas in South East Queensland—for example the Gold Coast and Ipswich.

While Cyril had outridden his claim on the country racing circuit, he was entitled to take a 3kg claim should he ride on city tracks. In October of 1976, Cyril ventured north to Brisbane on two occasions to take advantage of that claim. The first time he had one ride at Eagle Farm that ran unplaced and the following week he had one ride at Doomben on a horse called Bonford, and they came third. That racing season brought a few milestones Cyril's way. At Lismore on 16 April 1977, Cyril rode his one-hundredth winner on a horse called Clever Morgan. Then, on 20 July, Cyril won the South Grafton Cup, an open handicap, on 33/1 ($34) shot Badour, which still holds the record as the longest priced winner of that race.

By October 1977, Cyril had 113 wins beside his name and still had more than two years to serve of his apprenticeship. It was time for him to broaden his horizons long term, and to do that he needed to look further afield. The only way he could capitalise on his 3kg claim was to move to the city and work towards getting rides there. Cyril enquired about transferring his indentures from Mr Rayner to highly respected master of apprentices, Theo Green in Sydney, but Mr Green's stable of apprentices was full.

On 15 October, Cyril went to Eagle Farm for two rides. The young jockey had a much better outcome this time around riding against the bigwigs in the city, and came away with a win on Swift Phantom and a second on Bonford. On 5 November 1977, Cyril's indentures were transferred to astute Brisbane trainer Jim Marshall and Cyril moved into the downstairs section of Mr Marshall's family home in Hendra.

Cyril's first several weeks riding in Brisbane were mostly uneventful. But his nerves of steel and measured disposition would hold him in good stead when at the age of 18, he rode All Rainbows (owned by wealthy businessman John C Needham) to win at Eagle Farm for his new master and pull off one of the biggest betting plunges in Queensland racing history. That was Christmas Eve 1977. As much as 150/1 ($151) was bet about the mare that went to the post at 11/2 ($6.50). Bookmakers estimated that there was $100,000 in cash lifted from the Eagle Farm betting ring that day.

The final two years of Cyril's apprenticeship were not as rewarding as he would have liked. He didn't get the quality of rides he was hoping for and therefore the winners weren't as forthcoming. He had hoped to outride his claim in the city but that didn't happen. He didn't know it then, but there were much bigger racing thrills ahead for Cyril than outriding his claim in the city.

* * *

I met Cyril on 23 October 1982 at a nightclub called Sibyls on Adelaide Street in Brisbane. I was 17. At some point in the evening, a fellow was keenly chatting up my girlfriend and thought I needed some company. He said to me in a slurred voice, 'Come and meet my friend Cheryl'.

'I'm good thanks, I don't need to meet Cheryl,' I said to him.

With that, he picked me up and carried me over to a young man sitting on his own on a lounge overlooking the dance floor below us. He placed me on his lap and said, 'This is Cheryl'.

I got up straightaway, apologised to 'Cheryl' and walked away. The young man got to his feet and followed me and asked me to dance. He introduced himself to me, his name was Cyril. I found Cyril to be a lovely person, very quiet but kind and considerate—a gentleman really. Over time, our friendship turned into love and by 1984 we were inseparable.

By the time the 1984/85 racing season got underway, Cyril had built a respectable living as a senior jockey. He was stable jockey for astute trainer Evan Hartley and the combination enjoyed much success with Brilliant Beauty, Aunt Jane and Roman Knight all winning at Eagle Farm. Roman Knight was part-owned by Cyril's father Bob and the combination would go on to win the time-honoured Cleveland Bay Handicap in Townsville in the July of '85.

Cyril had also built a good clientele of trainers outside of Evan's stable with whom he was enjoying success. Those trainers included Bruce McLachlan, Barry Miller, Kelso Wood, John Fitzgerald, Jim Griffiths, Cobby Skinner, Ron Dillon, Brian Wakefield Sr, Bill Calder, Cyril's best mate Kevin Vizer, and Cyril's father Bob. Cyril's younger brother Warren, who was a star apprentice on the Northern Rivers before weight got the better of him, would soon be added to the list. Cyril was riding mostly on the Eagle Farm, Doomben, Ipswich and the Gold Coast circuit.

Importantly, Cyril got the job done for Vic on Rode Rouge, helping the colt overcome his barrier problems. In the June of '85

Rode Rouge lived up to his promise, winning a feature two-year-old race at Doomben over 1350 metres with Cyril in the saddle. That day he beat On Our Selection who ran second and Canny Lass who ran unplaced. Another important event took place during that period: Vic and Debby got engaged.

CHAPTER 3

FROM ERKY TO ATHLETE

By the time August '85 came around, Erky had been in a large paddock with 30 other horses for eight months. It was now time for him to return to Vic's stables. Debby and Vic broke him in but when it came to riding him, Debby was legged up because Erky was still not a strong horse at that time and Vic was too heavy. Debby says of the horse, 'He was a very dopey horse, I had to use spurs on him just to get him to trot and canter.' Debby rode him for three or four weeks before he went back out to Bobby Gill's property and was placed in a yard for six weeks.

Soon after, in September of that year, Vic took Rode Rouge to Melbourne. With Cyril riding him, they finished third in a three-year-old race at Moonee Valley. Vic and Cyril went on to enjoy good success with Rode Rouge winning races at Eagle Farm in February of '86, Toowoomba in March and Doomben in June.

Back to Erky, and at the end of the six weeks, Jeff received a phone call from Bobby Gill, telling him to come and pick up his horse. He was ready to go on with. Jeff drove down to the farm to inspect his horse, but there was a bit of a problem—Jeff couldn't find Erky in the paddock.

Jeff walked around and found Bobby and said, 'Bobby, where's that horse? I can't find him.'

Bobby replied with a cigarette hanging out the side of his mouth, 'He's over there in them yards.'

Jeff went back over to the yards. There were quite a few horses there, but Jeff remembered that Erky had a small white marking on one of his hind feet. It was that marking that allowed him to identify his horse.

Jeff immediately called Vic and Debby and told them, 'You better get down here to Bobby's and see this horse.'

Vic and Debby went straight down, taking the horse float with them. They both walked around and couldn't find the horse either. Debby recalls, 'At first, we couldn't find him. We didn't recognise the horse. He had grown that much you wouldn't have thought it could be the same horse.'

Erky had thrived at the Gill's dairy farm and in doing so, had undergone a major physical transformation under the Queensland sun. Erky loved nothing more than munching on his favourite treats, pineapple skins, beetroot skins, and brewer's grain. The Gill farm would become his home away from home where he would return to spell after each preparation, and he would leave there in the summer months with a yellow sunburnt coat.

At the beginning of the 1985/86 racing season, Erky was officially an early two-year-old and surprisingly, he had grown into a nice young athlete. Having been broken in and his education well underway, the young horse had also been named. There is a long-held belief among the racing fraternity that the owners made an error when naming Vo, that he was meant to be called Vo Rouge and carry on the Rouge name after Rode. That's not the case. The naming of Rode Rouge was an error. He was meant to be called Rode Road in reference to the main road that runs from McDowall through to Nundah in the northern suburbs of Brisbane.

Jeff explains that, 'The horse was never ever to be named anything except Vo Rogue. And I will tell you how I got it. His mother was Vow. You got the VO or Ivor, iVOr that's where we got the VO from. Now the Rogue, Vow's mother was Rogue River. That's how the ROGUE came. VO ROGUE. John Murray wanted to name him Axe Attack, but by the time he came up with that name he was too late. I had already named him.'

It was time for the newly-named Vo Rogue, who had also earned a stable name change from Erky to Vo, to be educated out of the barriers.

Jeff and Vic took the horse to the Gold Coast. 'They used to have those short jump outs just down the straight,' recalls Jeff. 'Vo drew number one barrier. When they jumped, one of Jim Griffiths' horses came across and hit Vo and he put him into the rail. He nearly jumped the inside fence. Vo finished 15 lengths behind the second-last horse. I was gobsmacked wondering what had happened. Before the trial, Vicky said this horse will win this jump out by 15 lengths. Vicky said that the outside horse had knocked him down. Not intentionally, but you know how they jump, he's come across.'

That experience did not sit well with Vo. 'We had a lot of trouble with him for four or five months after that', Jeff explains, 'Vo would stand in the barriers and watch the other horses jump and then he would jump behind them.'

Jeff and Vic took Vo to the Gold Coast jump outs every Tuesday to try to rectify the matter but were unsuccessful. With Cyril riding Rode Rouge and other horses in Vic's stable, he was asked to ride Vo in jump outs at Doomben. Cyril was able to give Vo the confidence he needed. Before long, rather than being the last to jump out of the barriers, Vo was the first.

On 18 January 1986, Vo had his first race start at the Gold Coast in a two-year-old maiden over 1110 metres on a track rated a Good 3[1].

---

1 Track ratings describe the firmness of the surface of a racetrack. Terminology has changed over the years and Racing Australia has amended their records to reflect current terminology which is used in this book. However, some sections of the book also refer to the old terminologies. There are 10 track ratings from a Firm 1 (formerly Fast 1) to a Heavy 10. A Dead track rating (now termed a Good 4 of a Soft 5) described a surface that was slightly rain effected and had give in it. A Slow track rating (now termed Soft 6 or Soft 7) is more rain affected and the track chops up and can shift underfoot.

He ran sixth of 11 and was beaten 11.6 lengths. Cyril was the jockey on that occasion. At his next three starts, Vo was ridden by Gavin Birrer when second of 12 over 800 metres at the Gold Coast (Good 3), Les Harris when ninth of 10 over 1110 metres at the Gold Coast (Soft 7), and Les Harris again when eleventh of 12 at Doomben over 1200 metres (Good 3). Vo was beaten a total of 36.4 lengths across those three events.

Cyril rode the winner of the Doomben event. It was a two-year-old maiden race on 16 April and Cyril won it on Spirit of Bengal for his best mate Kevin Vizer. I remember Kevie proudly displaying the winning photo on a wall in his house. He was always so keen to point out where Vo finished in the race, almost 14.5 lengths behind his horse. After that race, Vo had a two-and-a-half-month break from racing before his fifth race start when Cyril would ride him again.

There was much confidence among the Team about the horse going into his fifth race start, a two-year-old maiden over 1200 metres at Eagle Farm on 25 June 1986 on a track rated a Firm 2. Firstly, Vic had called in equine chiropractor Paul Brady to go over the horse. Vo's previous runs had been well below what was expected of the horse and Vic was looking for answers. Mr Brady found them. Vo's seventh cervical vertebra had 'popped out', potentially a result from a fall when Vo was a foal. Mr Brady worked wonders on the horse and was able to correct the problem which would be regularly checked throughout Vo's career. Secondly, blinkers were added as a gear change to help Vo focus better in his races as he had been somewhat field-shy. Lastly, leading into the race, Cyril rode Vo in a solid track gallop on a slightly damp track at Doomben against his two-year-old stablemate Sirus, a dominant maiden winner at his previous race start. As Cyril puts it, 'Vo kicked Sirus' arse.'

The short break, chiropractic treatment, gear change and track gallop had done the horse a world of good. He was ready to step up—and step up he did.

In a field of 18, Vo drew barrier 12. He sat just off the pace in fourth and fifth positions. Rounding the home turn, he retained his position and at the 200-metre mark, Cyril let him go. He raced away and won by five lengths at the odds of 5/1 ($6). The bookies' bags were left a little lighter that day.

Soon after that win, Jeff moved Vo into the stables at Cyril's Hendra property and Vo remained there throughout his racing career whenever he was in work in Brisbane.

Cyril rode Vo at his next start, 16 August, when sixth of 11 in an Improvers over 1110 metres at the Gold Coast on a track rated a Soft 5. He finished 10.6 lengths behind the winner. Soon after Vo suffered a minor injury and had a rest. He commenced racing again on Melbourne Cup day, 4 November, at the Gold Coast. Ridden by Kenne Sawyers in an Improvers, he beat two home in an eight-horse field finishing seven and a half lengths from the winner on a tracked rated a Good 3. Debby was legged up at Vo's next two starts, both at the Sunshine Coast. On 15 November, Debby piloted Vo into second place in an Improvers over 1200 metres on a Good 3, but was then unplaced over 1300 metres on a Good 3 on 22 November 1986.

* * *

Outside of racing, Vo was a quirky horse. He was a windsucker and a weaver—that is, he would put his teeth into the stable door and suck in air, and he stood in his stable and swayed from side to side. He was quite happy for people to visit him and say hello, but he let you know when you had worn out your welcome. He would move away and proceed to ignore you.

Vo also had a habit of putting his feed into his water bucket. Jeff explains that Vo drank twice as much as most horses and would often run out of water using a normal-sized water bucket. Vo would take a mouthful of feed, then a mouthful of water and he would drag his water bucket through his stable. To overcome this problem, Jeff made Vo a bigger and stronger water bucket and hung it on the outside of his stable door, with the feed tin hung on the inside of the stable door.

To bust another myth, Vo was hosed and shampooed regularly like any other horse. The fictional story that was told from time to time was that Vo was never washed and that he smelled poorly because of it. That is not the case. Like any other horse, Vo did sweat, and he loved rolling around in the sand roll and doing horsey things. So of course he was hosed down and had his coat cleaned every day when he was in work.

Vo was always so excited when Jeff pulled into the driveway every afternoon. He knew the sound of Jeff's ute and when he heard it, he would start calling out, letting everyone know Jeff had arrived. It was an afternoon ritual, seven days a week, that Vo would take Jeff for a walk and stop where he wanted to pick. When he had had enough, Vo would lift his head, poke Jeff in the ribs and lead Jeff home. He was such a cool horse.

The ritual remained in place when Vo travelled. There was no missing Jeff and Vo, particularly at Flemington where the horse stabled at Phillip Burke's complex. More often than not, Jeff wore the stable uniform: T-shirt, stubbies and thongs, regardless of the weather. And Vo, well just typical Vo Rogue style really, he led the way and Jeff followed.

CHAPTER 4

FIRST TRIP TO MELBOURNE

At the end of 1986, Cyril copped a three-month suspension at the Gold Coast for running and handling on a horse called Bold Elf trained by Kelso Wood. Cyril refuted the charge and had the time reduced to two months on appeal. A worker for the Wood stable told Cyril the horse was retired after its next start as it wasn't deemed good enough to be a racehorse. That didn't help Cyril's cause.

The last horse Cyril rode before commencing his suspension was Vo. That was on 15 December 1986 at Murwillumbah, a country track in the Northern Rivers. The rain tumbled down on that day as Cyril travelled from Brisbane with Vic. Cyril suggested to Vic that he turn the car and float around and go home; the horse would not perform on a wet track. But they continued their journey and Vo and Cyril finished fourth of 10 in an Improvers race over 1000 metres on a track rated a Heavy 10. They were beaten just over two and a half lengths.

Vo had four starts after that race at Murwillumbah for three wins—two at the Gold Coast and one at Doomben. In between those wins was a fifth placing at the Gold Coast. He was ridden in all four races by Larry Allen. It was about that time that Ray Murrihy became the new Chairman of Stewards for thoroughbred racing in Queensland. Ray remembers well the first time he came across Vic. In fact, it was his first day in his new job.

Ray recalls his colleague Tom Murphy telling him that he had a matter to deal with regarding a trainer called Vic Rail. Vic was arguing the point over a horse he had entered in a race; however, the horse was an ineligible entry. Mr Murphy had a one-minute egg timer on his desk in the stewards room and he said to Vic, 'You have one minute to state your case.'

With that, Mr Murphy turned the timer upside down to commence the countdown.

'Vic gave his opinions on racing stewards, race clubs, the State Premier and even the Pope got a mention,' Ray says.

All to no avail as the outcome was that Vic was fined $50.

Ray quickly became aware that Vic had permission for his team of 20-plus horses to race barefooted, including Vo Rogue. The Australian Rules of Racing state that horses must wear aluminium racing plates or at a minimum, racing tips when competing in races and barrier trials. Racing Rule AR 107 (2) states, 'in exceptional circumstances the stewards may permit a horse to run barefooted or partly shod'.

Although Vic was a farrier by trade, he had raced and trialled all his horses barefooted over a period of 15 years as a trainer. Vic didn't believe horses needed shoes and Vo was no exception. He had not previously worn shoes or race plates. In fact, Vo had raced 14 times, all barefooted and had won four races. He was showing enormous promise.

Ray could see no reason why Vic should not comply with the Australian Rules of Racing, and therefore, couldn't see why Vic's horses should run without racing plates or at the bare minimum, racing tips. 'Vic was also a farrier and shod the horses of other trainers,' says Ray. 'I told Vic that he would have to comply with the rule and that included Vo Rogue.'

Vic said to him, 'What if he can't perform wearing tips or shoes?' 'What if he becomes a champion?' Ray responded.

Vic was not happy with Ray's directive and later told journalist Tony Meany of *The Sun* newspapers that, 'Tommy [Woodcock] never shod his horses and it makes sense … Once officials see a horse who is pretty good, they start taking notice and realise not having shoes is out of the ordinary. You only have to look at trotters. Their shoes have to be specially balanced. Disturb that balance and it alters the gait of the horse. It only stands to reason that putting shoes on racehorses will affect their action as well.'

Vic and Jeff decided to take Vo to Melbourne and have a crack at some of the three-year-old races in the Autumn Carnival of 1987 Rode Rouge accompanied them. At that time, Vo had accumulated $11,000 worth of prize money in his bank account. Larry Allen was invited to go with the Team but he declined—Larry had his sights set on winning the Gold Coast premiership, a feat he duly achieved for the second year in succession.

Once in Melbourne, Vic had no choice but to adhere to the Australian racing rule about racing plates and tips, and so, on race day, Vo wore racing tips on all four hooves. Vic tacked them onto his hooves on race morning and took them off soon after each race. However, Vic trialled Rode Rouge barefooted and one of the trainer's dobbed him into the stewards. Vic was fined $200 for his, shall we say, lapse in memory.

Vo initially had mixed results racing in Melbourne. At his first start, he finished third in the Listed Debonair Stakes over 1400 metres at Flemington for jockey David Tootell on a track rated a Firm 2. At his third start he finished second to the Colin Hayes trained Military Plume in the Group 1 Australian Guineas over 1600 metres at Flemington. Colin Hayes was then, and still is today, considered one of the most influential and successful racehorse trainers in the history of Australian racing, alongside Tommy Smith and Bart Cummings.

Brian York rode Vo in the Australian Guineas and again the track was rated a Firm 2. Jeff recalls Brian telling him that if he had ridden Vo before the Australian Guineas and knew what he could do, he would have won. The day after the Guineas, an offer to purchase Vo for the sum of $130,000 was made by the Bruce McLachlan stable, for whom Brian was stable rider. The offer was refused. Slotted between the Debonair Stakes and Australian Guineas achievements was a tenth of twelve in the Group 3 Autumn Stakes at Sandown over 1400 metres when ridden by John Scorse, and again, the track was rated a Firm 2.

I clearly remember his fourth run which was in the Listed Autumn Classic at Caulfield over 1800 metres. John Scorse was again in the saddle but on that day, the track was rated a Heavy 10. The race was run on 28 February 1987. Cyril and I were married two weeks earlier on Valentine's Day and after spending our honeymoon on Dunk Island, we made our way down to Cyril's father Bob's grazing property in Wyan, about 30 minutes southwest of Casino.

The Casino races were on and Cyril told me he was keen to go and watch 'a horse go around in Melbourne', on the racecourse TV screens. As the start time for the race approached, I asked Cyril what horse he was interested in watching. He said, 'Vo Rogue'. I looked across at the bookies stands and he was reasonably long odds. Officially he started at 16/1 ($17). I asked Cyril if I should back him and he said, 'No, he can't win today.'

As the field approached the turn, Vo was leading and looked to be going well within himself. I turned to Cyril and said, 'I thought you said he can't win?'

'He can't,' Cyril responded. 'He hasn't let him go yet. As soon as he gives him his head, he will go backwards.'

And that's exactly what happened. The record books will show that Vo was beaten 16.7 lengths, and I learned what Cyril and the Vo Rogue Team already knew: Vo couldn't handle a wet track. As time would tell, he couldn't even handle a drop of water on the track. The harder the track, the better Vo raced. It would soon become clear that water was Vo's kryptonite.

After that race, Jeff suggested to Vic that they were better off getting a jockey that they knew and asked Vic what his thoughts were on that. Vic's response was, 'Cyril should be coming back in a week's time, see if you can get him to come down.'

Jeff called Cyril and asked him to come to Melbourne to ride Vo in the Creswick Stakes over 2000 metres on Monday 9 March at Flemington, and stay down for the following Saturday to ride him in the Group 2 Alister Clark Stakes over 2040 metres at Moonee Valley. We had not long returned from our honeymoon and Cyril was a bit on the heavy side. Vo had 55kg in the Creswick and 54kg in the Alister Clark.

Cyril said to Jeff, 'How about I just come down and ride him on the Saturday?'

'A number of leading riders have been ringing for the rides including Michael Clarke [Victoria's then-leading jockey], he wants to ride him in both races,' Jeff replied.

Cyril quickly responded, 'I'll see you Monday, pick me up at the airport.'

When Cyril got off the phone, he put his sweat gear on and headed off on foot towards Nudgee Road. A few hours later he called me from a phone box at the top end of Gerler Road, about two kilometres from home, and asked me to come and pick him up. He was buggered. For the next week, Cyril literally worked his butt off to get his weight down.

I had met Jeff many times, just casually, and knew him as 'Froggy'; however, at the time of Cyril's first race ride in Melbourne, I wouldn't say I knew him well at all. I would mostly see Jeff and speak to him when he was out and about with a brown horse on a long lead rope. As it turned out, that horse was Vo. At that time, I wasn't aware of the depth of the association that Cyril had formed with Jeff and Vic, or the work Cyril had put into Vo's education. Cyril didn't say a lot about the horses he was riding or working with, and still doesn't.

I accompanied Cyril to Melbourne and stayed for a few days. I was just so excited to be going to Flemington—it was such a treat for me. I couldn't wait for the day to begin so I could watch a live hurdle race, see the horses race down the famous straight six, and get a close-up, in the flesh look at one of my favourite horses at that time, the New Zealand champion Bonecrusher, who was racing in the Group 1 Australian Cup later that day. Of course, I was very proud that Cyril was riding at Flemington that day too.

Cyril wasn't daunted as he headed into the jockey's room. For Cyril, riding at Flemington represented just another day at the office—only on that day, that office was hosting some of the best racehorses, trainers and jockeys in Australasia for one of Victoria's premier Group 1 events. For that reason, the eyes of the racing public were set firmly on it, as was that of the press.

Inside the jockeys' room it was a who's who of the racing world. Legendary New Zealand jockey Bob Skelton MBE, four time Melbourne Cup winning jockey Harry White, Victoria's premier rider and Melbourne Cup winner Michael Clarke, and Manikato's famous jockey Gary Willetts were among the headline acts. They all welcomed the stranger from Queensland.

I remember feeling nervous as I sat in the grandstand to watch the Creswick Stakes, binoculars always focused on Cyril and Vo as they paraded behind the barriers. I was hoping that Cyril and Vo didn't have the knots in their stomachs that I had in mine. I should have known better. More than nine years had passed since Cyril pulled of one of the biggest plunges in Queensland racing history. He was now 28 and had a wealth of experience behind him. His nerves had never faltered, and his disposition was as measured as ever. And Vo, as I would learn, was the ultimate professional. Still, I really had no clue what I was about to witness or the ride of a lifetime that was about to commence for all of us who were connected with Vo.

The barriers opened and Cyril took Vo to the lead—or, as I found out later, Vo took Cyril. But they weren't just a few lengths in front of the field, Vo and Cyril were in one race and the other 18 horses were in another. They must have been as much as 20 lengths in front of the next horse at one stage of the race. I remember thinking, *What the hell are you doing? No horse can sustain that speed over 2000 metres.* But what I didn't know at the time was that Vo was no ordinary horse. He was a superstar in the making and anyone at Flemington that day would have realised that.

The punters who took the odds of 4/1 ($5) never had any worries about collecting. Vo had over eight lengths to spare on the line to the second horse, War Correspondent, and he ran the journey in a blistering 2-00.7, a new metric track record. Four races later, Bonecrusher won the Australian Cup also over 2000 metres in 2-05.60, almost five seconds slower that Vo's winning time.

An old timer once told me that at gallop speed, one second is equivalent to a six-length margin. Imagine what a spectacle that would have been had Vo been in the 1987 Australian Cup and beaten Bonecrusher by 30 lengths? Twelve months later, Vo would be the headline act with Bonecrusher in the 1988 Bicentenary Australian Cup, but more on that later.

On the Wednesday, we all ventured to Kyneton where Cyril and Rode Rouge finished fourth. I then returned to Brisbane after the race as my annual leave was up and I had to go back to work. The next day, Cyril went to trackwork at Moonee Valley to ride Vo in his final workout for Saturday's race, but Vic left Cyril in the grandstand, preferring to ride him himself.

Vic's preferred footwear when riding trackwork was a pair of gumboots. I have no idea what the Victorian stewards thought about Vic wearing gumboots while riding trackwork, but Ray Murrihy took a dim view. 'Vic had some good points but agreeing with officialdom was not one of them,' says Ray, who describes Vic as having a confrontational attitude. Ray recalls castigating Vic for riding trackwork in gumboots. 'I did not approve of Vic wearing rubber boots to ride trackwork in and I told Vic that he could no longer wear them,' Ray says. 'Vic told me there was nowhere in the rule book that stated that he couldn't wear rubber boots.' Ray adds that one of the trainers in Brisbane suggested to Ray soon after that when the rule book was written, no one ever thought there would be a Vic Rail. 'Vic was certainly different,' Ray remarks.

It's a good thing for Vic that Ray was not Chairman of Stewards a few years earlier when Vic's trackwork attire most certainly did not meet what would be accepted as safe workwear. Vic sometimes rode in what he called his 'Chinese riding boots', aka rubber thongs. His skull cap or riding helmet was actually a motorbike helmet shaped like a bowl. It didn't have a chin strap, so Vic used electric wire and threaded that through and tied it off to the side. Yes, Vic was certainly different, but may I add, creative. As far as Vic was concerned, helmets were only useful if you fell off and he had no intention of falling off.

On Saturday 14 March, Vo stepped out in the Group 2 Alister Clark Stakes at Moonee Valley over 2040 metres, the same distance as the WS Cox Plate, Australia's premier Group 1 Weight For Age (WFA) event. Vo once again blitzed the opposition, going straight to the front and prevailing by two and a half lengths to the Colin Hayes-trained Cossack Warrior. This time, Vo ran a new track record time of 2-03.4 which was 0.4 seconds faster than brilliant colt Red Anchor's effort in the 1985 WS Cox Plate when ridden by champion jockey Mick Dittman. Mick once told me that Red Anchor was the best horse he ever rode throughout his long and distinguished career, which was duly acknowledged in 2002 when Mick was inducted into the Australian Racing Hall of Fame.

Cyril came home that night after winning the Alister Clark Stakes, with two bunches of roses with him—one red and one pink. The red roses were a part of the trophies for the winning owner and the pink bunch was the trophy for the winning jockey. Cyril delivered the roses to Jeff's wife Sandra the next day. Cyril was pretty chuffed because Jacki MacDonald (aka Jacki Mac) was on the flight home and commented to Cyril how beautiful the roses were. She even gave him a tip on how to keep them fresh for longer. For those of you that don't remember her, Jacki co-compered *Hey Hey, It's Saturday* with Daryl Somers in the 1980s, along with doing a lot of other television and radio work. Watching *Hey Hey, It's Saturday* on a Saturday night was a ritual for many Australians before venturing out for the night.

But I digress, again, and after dazzling wins in Melbourne, Team Vo moved north to Sydney and attempted the Canterbury Guineas and Rosehill Guineas races for three-year-olds. The first race on 21 March was run on a Soft 5 track and Vo failed to beat a runner home. The next race was run on 4 April on a Firm 2 and Vo beat one runner home. Vo had had enough. It was time for the young star to return to Bobby Gill's dairy farm to chew on brewer's grain and pineapple and beetroot skins under the autumn sun. And so, Team Vo headed home.

* * *

With an exciting Autumn Carnival behind them, and Vo in early preparation for the 1987 Melbourne Spring Racing Carnival, Jeff acquired a young gelding, whose education at the barrier Cyril was assisting with. I remember the horse so well. His name was Bitoney and he was one of the most beautiful horses you could ever see. He looked like the horse from the movie *The Black Stallion*. He was simply magnificent. The horse would eventually accompany Vo to Melbourne in the spring of 1988. Cyril won a race on Bitoney at Kilmore in the September of that year.

On one particular afternoon, Jeff was out the front of our property giving Vo a pick of grass. Vo was happy to hang around our place that day.

I said to Jeff, 'How did your horse go at the barriers today?'

Jeff replied with words similar to, but not as kind as, 'Why don't you ask your idiot husband?'

Cyril overheard our conversation and made a retort. Very quickly, a verbal stoush erupted and Jeff and Cyril exchanged several unpleasantries toward one another. As it happened, the horse did not do well in his education at the barriers that morning. Cyril blamed Jeff's team of helpers and was of the opinion they should have just got out of the way and let him do his job. Jeff felt differently and put the blame squarely on Cyril's shoulders. They told each other exactly what they could do with themselves, and Cyril went inside the house. I followed him and said to him, 'You will go back outside and apologise to Jeff.'

'No I won't. I'm not at fault, he is,' Cyril replied

'I don't care. You can apologise anyway. Jesus Christ Cyril, he owns Vo Rogue. You can't risk him taking you off,' I replied.

Cyril assured me Jeff would not take him off, saying, 'We've said what we had to say to each other, it's over and it won't be discussed again.' And it wasn't. Their friendship and professional relationship carried on as if that incident never happened. And I think that is a measure of the man Jeff Perry is, along with Cyril. And it's a good thing too. Jeff would have had no problems whatsoever finding a replacement jockey.

We later became aware that many high-profile jockeys across Australia were calling Vic and Jeff on a regular basis for the ride.

'There were a few in Melbourne who wanted to ride him. Michael Clarke, he wanted to ride him. I could have got Harry [White] any time.' Jeff says.

Vic also had a long standing friendship with another Melbourne Cup winning jockey, Mel Schumacher. Sometime after the first Melbourne assault, Vic and Debby moved into the house beside ours. Mel and his wife Pam were regular visitors to Vic and Debby's, and their son Clayton helped out in Vic's stables. Mel was keen to throw his leg over Vo and take the reins. Jeff told me that on more than one occasion Vic's stable approached Jeff and put the question to him of Mel riding Vo. On each occasion Jeff responded with a firm 'No'.

'Most probably, if I was going to go down that way and change the jockey, most probably I would have gone Harry's way,' says Jeff. But for Jeff, he had his jockey: Vo and Cyril gelled, they got each other and that was that.

Vic would later tell Rod Gallegos who reported for the *Telegraph* that, 'Cyril is the most underrated jockey in Brisbane and he's been riding Vo Rogue since he was a baby.'

The jockeys weren't the only one's circling. Trainers had their fingers on the dial as well, including the legendary Tommy Smith who Jeff used to casually strap for when he brought his horses to Brisbane. Jeff was criticised in some circles for leaving Vo with Vic and Cyril who were deemed in the press as 'the unfashionable trainer–jockey combination'. Jeff stuck solid though. As far as he was concerned, Vic and Cyril had done nothing wrong and Team Vo had a bond more important than money.

CHAPTER 5

THE SPRING OF '87

Vo had one firm goal in the spring of '87: the WS Cox Plate at Moonee Valley on 24 October. He was the track record holder for the distance at Moonee Valley and Team Vo had their eyes set firmly on the prize.

Vo's trek towards the main event started with a bang on 29 August. He bolted in in the TAB Silver Anniversary Handicap over 1200 metres at Doomben on a Firm 2 track at the lucrative odds of 4/1. He ran 1-09.7. He put in a repeat performance at his next start, just one week later in the Ipswich Fourex Flying over 1200 metres on a track rated a Good 3. The bookies had learned their lesson and he went to the post at 7/4 ($2.75). Soon after, Vo was on a float being towed by Jeff, with Vic in the passenger's seat—destination: Melbourne.

Vo's first start was in the Group 2 John F Feehan Stakes (WFA) over 1619 metres at Moonee Valley on a track rated a Good 3. Vo didn't lead that day. He travelled second behind Lake Worth with the great stallion Rubiton sitting behind him in third. As Lake Worth dropped off, Vo surged to the lead. But he couldn't hold off Rubiton, who was taking all before him in his racing career. Vo was beaten less than one and a half lengths into second place. Rubiton, ridden by Harry White and trained by Pat Barns, ran a race record, and although he ran an extra 19 metres with the moveable rail being out, he still equalled the track record for 1600 metres. Vo was not disgraced in running second.

Vo suffered another defeat at his next race start when third in the Listed Royal Show Handicap over 1800 metres at Caulfield. Vo carried 59kg and sat back in fourth place in the running. As the race progressed, he moved to the outside of the leaders, but he couldn't hold off Tristram and Real Purpose with the margins being a nose by a head.

Following those defeats, it was back to what would become Vo's favourite track, Flemington, and the Group 2 Turnbull Stakes over 2000 metres on a track rated a Good 3. The date was 3 October. On this day, racing fans got their first glimpse of the lion heart that lay within Vo's soul.

The barriers opened, Vo went to the lead and he set a blistering pace. Vo had it all his own way in front until the 200-metre mark when stallion Fair Sir emerged from the pack and ran to Vo. At his past two starts Vo had been run down over shorter journeys, but on this day he staged a battle royale with Fair Sir who was a the topline West Australian galloper. Fair Sir was a Group 1 and Group 2 winner in Perth, and runner up in the Group 1 Underwood Stakes at his previous start.

Fair Sir looked like he might run straight past Vo, but Vo fought on. It quickly became east versus west, the two horses head-to-head, stride for stride, with their jockeys throwing everything they could at their courageous warriors. As they drew to the line Vo had a head to spare over Fair Sir who was oh so brave in defeat. The time was 2-01.3—only 0.6 seconds outside Vo's own record. For Cyril, it represented Vo's best effort to date, and he was just so very proud of him. Vic told anyone who would listen that Vo wasn't fit, he had won the race on heart. Vo had a lion's heart, ever hungry for another win.

The next week Vo lined up in the Group 1 Elders Mile at Caulfield. He started 4/1 favourite but was upstaged by 25/1 ($26) shot Caledonian Boy, a rank failure at its previous start in the Marlboro

Cup at the same track. The margin was a long neck, and the time was once again sizzling, 1-35.9—only 0.2 seconds outside the track record.

It was now 24 October and the WS Cox Plate Day of 1987 had arrived. The main event gathered together one of the best fields ever assembled for that race. It was without question the best field Vo had encountered to date; but despite that, my confidence in Vo winning was high. I remember how excited we all were when Vo drew barrier one for the race. Cyril's intention was to lead at a comfortable tempo, but even the best laid plans can go astray.

When the field jumped, Vo took up the lead by two lengths, but the New Zealand mare Tidal Light came across from the outside barrier and tried to head him off. Vo fired up badly and took off.

Cyril tried his best to settle him. Vo's head was noticeably held high as they went into the turn out of the straight. Vo was tugging hard for more rein. At the 1200-metre mark, Vo was still pulling and had gone out by over eight lengths to Tidal Light with another eight lengths to Marwong who was travelling in third place at that point of the race. Even that far out the red-hot tempo of the race suggested the winner would be the new track record holder for the distance.

With 600 metres to go, Vo was still four lengths in front of Marwong who had improved around the tiring Tidal Light, but the cavalry was coming. And it was coming quickly.

On the point of the turn Vo was battling ever so courageously as only he knew how, but Our Poetic Prince was coming at high speed and had the better of him. As they straightened for home, Our Poetic Prince skipped away and looked to have a winning break. Rubiton was hitting top speed, and as he did that, he stumbled and bumped into Fair Sir who was making his run with Rubiton. Harry White, riding Rubiton, quickly balanced his horse. Rubiton let down with enormous strength and surged past Our Poetic Prince in the final 30 metres to win the race by a long neck. Fair Sir was a further length away in third place and Vo a length behind him in fourth place. The fifth horse, Beau Zam, finished one and a half lengths behind Vo.

Rubiton smashed Vo's record by half a second. He ran 2-02.9, but it was well-acknowledged that Vo's scorching pace was a major factor in setting up Rubiton's new track record time.

I remember sitting in the grandstand immediately after the race thinking, *What just happened? No, no, no, that's not how the story ends. Vo was meant to win the race, not Rubiton. We need to run it again, this time without Tidal Light.*

Well, that was never going to happen.

It's hard to say if the result would have been any different though. Rubiton and Vo met three times in their racing careers and Rubiton beat Vo every time. Rubiton went on to win the Group 1 MacKinnon Stakes (WFA) over 2000 metres at Flemington one week later. He didn't race again due to a tendon injury that he acquired when getting ready for the autumn of '88, and he retired to stud duties.

In a career that spanned just 16 race starts, Rubiton amassed 10 wins, four at Group 1 level and three at Group 2, plus one second and four thirds. He was a true champion on the track and those qualities carried over to his stud career. He sired many outstanding stakes winners, my favourite being Fields of Omagh who won the WS Cox Plate twice, in 2003 and 2006.

Cyril and the Team maintained they would have loved to have met Rubiton in the autumn of '88 when Vo came of age. Some in the industry even suggested that Rubiton was retired because the word around the tracks was that Vo had grown an extra set of legs and would be the dominant racehorse moving forward. I don't know about that. What I do know is that had Rubiton not injured his tendon and subsequently retired, there sure would have been some great duels between them. But we can only ponder those results.

Vo's campaign for that preparation finished unexpectantly back in Queensland. Vic and Jeff were caught unawares when they went to nominate Vo for the MacKinnon Stakes, only to find that nominations had closed the week before. What was a disappointment for the Team became a coup for the Brisbane Turf Club.

With no time to waste, Vo was on the float heading back to Brisbane to compete in the Lord Mayor's Cup at Doomben over 2020 metres on 31 October. However, with a big campaign behind him and carrying 59kg, Vo, the even money favourite ($2), went down by a head to the Mick Mair-trained Burglar of Bamff, ridden by Lloyd Brazier. From his eight starts that campaign, Vo had three wins, three seconds, a third and a fourth.

Vo had earned his spell, one which would see him mature into much more than an above-average racehorse. Those long days spent basking in the hot Queensland sunshine at Bobby Gill's property would see the now four-year-old emerge a superstar.

CHAPTER 6

A LEGEND IS BORN

Things were very different for Vic and Cyril as they readied themselves for the autumn of '88. Although they had competed with Rode Rouge that one time at Moonee Valley in the spring of 1985, they didn't make the same impact then as they did with Vo across 1987.

In Queensland, Vic and Cyril were well-known in the racing industry and Cyril also had a strong following from many on the Northern Rivers. In Victoria however, it was a different story.

In the autumn of '87, the broadcasters, punters and other racing folk found the name Vic Rail rather amusing because the Victorian Railway system is known as The Vic Rail and there were numerous comments made about that. Would you believe that for some time Vic and Debby also lived in Railway Parade at Clayfield, and the only job Vic's father William ever had was working for the railway?

As for Cyril, the Victorians had no idea who C Small was. He was called Chris Small or Craig Small. But with record breaking wins by Vo in the autumn and courageous efforts by him across the spring of '87, the names Vic Rail and Cyril Small had become familiar names in Victoria.

Vic in particular was well-liked by the Victorian racing community and punting public. He was a believable battler and I think they liked that about him. He had a lot of lines on his face which made him look older than his 42 years. He had widened around the girth, and he often referred to his bigger belly as a dropped chest. Vic never subscribed to the ethos of keeping up appearances. When he wasn't in a suit for race day, he wore the stable uniform of a T-shirt, stubbies and thongs.

Vic had a penchant for changing his hairstyle regularly between a perm and a slicked back look. Soon after he got his first perm, Vic ran into his old boss Jim Griffiths. Vic always called him 'Boss', or Mr Griffiths. Debby told me that Mr Griffiths commented to Vic, 'Vic if I didn't know better, I'd think you'd gone a bit girly. But I'd hate to be the poor bastard who came up behind you and touched you on the arse.'

Vic loved a chat and was always at ease when holding court with the punting public, the press, and later politicians and other affluent admirers. That suited Cyril because while he was and has always been very accommodating with people and the press, he was and still is rather reserved and happy for the spotlight to shine anywhere but on him.

Elite journalist Les Carlyon would later write of Cyril in *The Age* newspaper, 'And Cyril Small, the Rogue's jockey, still appears and disappears like some quiet hit-man from interstate. You see him in a suit about an hour before the race; he is back in it half-an-hour later. He takes no other rides, and is disinclined to rave about the Rogue or himself.'

The autumn of '88 would change everything. The names Vic Rail and Cyril Small would not just become familiar, they would become forever etched into the Australian racing history books, courtesy of an extraordinary brown horse often described as plain. But in reality, Vo Rogue was anything but plain.

* * *

Vo had a spectacular start to the autumn of '88 which commenced in the Group 1 William Reid Stakes (WFA) at Moonee Valley over 1200 metres. Run on Australia Day that year, the connections used the race as a barrier trial for the horse in preparation for his campaign that would culminate with the Australian Cup over 2000 metres, also run under WFA conditions. The Australian Cup that year celebrated Australia's bicentenary and was run at Flemington on Monday 14 March.

After a brief spell, Vo trained at Nudgee Beach for four weeks—straight out of the paddock. He returned to the stable the day after Christmas. He had two short track gallops and a jump out behind him going into the Group 1 sprint. Some of the best sprinters in racing history have won the William Reid over the years including Winfreux (1968), Toy Show (1977) and Manikato five times (1979–83). In more recent years, the tradition continued with champions Apache Cat (2008 and 2009) and Black Caviar (2011 and 2013) victorious.

While fitness was of some concern, the connections expected the horse to be competitive. Jeff was confident his horse could win, because as Jeff puts it, 'We knew the horse could run a sub 1-10.0 over 1200 metres on a firm surface.'

However, there was no real confidence in the betting ring by the punting public and Vo's starting price was 11/2. When the barriers opened, Vo jumped to the front and that's where he stayed. On a track rated a Good 3, and with the clock stopping at a slick 1-09.9, Vo equalled the race record and had three quarters of a length to spare to Military Plume with Groucho third and Campaign King fourth. Some barrier trial it turned out to be, $130,000 jumped into kitty!

And it's fair to say, it was on that day that the Vo Rogue legend was born.

Soon after that race, we commissioned artist Rick Sinclair to paint a portrait of Vo and Cyril winning the William Reid. Rick had been displaying his art for some time at the Gold Coast Turf Club and his work was superb. Rick was very excited and he told us he couldn't sleep once he started the project. It took him 100 hours to complete the 1800mm x 1200mm oil on canvas painting. We think it is spectacular and the best painting we have ever seen.

Next up was the Group 2 CF Orr Stakes over 1400 metres at Sandown under WFA conditions on 6 February. Again, Vo competed against Military Plume with the latter going to the post a 5/4 ($2.25) favourite and Vo Rogue at 9/4 ($3.25). Vo was never in doubt at any time. At the 200-metre mark, legendary race caller Bill Collins excitedly declared, 'Oh he's got it won, he's walked in. Vic Rail's got this horse fit.' Vo had seven lengths to spare from King Phoenix second, Groucho third and nearly eight lengths behind Vo in fourth place was Military Plume. Vo ran an impressive 1-24.30 on a track rated a Good 3.

Soon after the CF Orr Stakes win, Jeff returned to Brisbane for the birth of his first child, daughter Cymone who was born on 11 February. While Jeff was in Brisbane, he asked a good friend of his to help Vic with the horse. At that time, Jeff thought that Vo would have two more runs prior to the Bicentenary Australian Cup. Those were to be the Group 2 Blamey Stakes over 1600 metres under WFA conditions at Flemington on 13 February, and the Group 2 St George Stakes at Caulfield over 1800 metres (WFA) on 27 February. The Group 1 Futurity Stakes over 1400 metres at Caulfield on 5 March had been pencilled in just in case Vo needed one more run to have him ready for the Cup, but it really wasn't on Jeff's radar. From the outset, his goal was the Australian Cup.

Vo went into his next race, the Blamey Stakes, as a 2/5 ($1.40) favourite on a track rated a Firm 2. The bookies were not taking any chances this time, and Vo now had a cult-like following among the punting ranks. Anyone who doubted that Vo was not the real deal had their mindset recalibrated that day.

Vo and Cyril were literally low-flying as they sped towards the winning post seven lengths ahead of Bonhomie, Cossack Warrior and King Phoenix. With no horses around him, Vo was left to race the clock on the giant semaphore board. Many in the crowd cheering him on started chanting the time: '29, 30, 31, 32, 33, 34.'

The clock stopped at 1-34.0, a new track record. Vo took 0.2 seconds off the previous record held by Amiable for no less than 48 years, one of the longest standing records in racing history.

Keith Hillier, Chief Racing Writer for *The Sun* newspaper, revealed that champion trainer Bart Cummings commented that there was not a horse in the world who could have beaten Vo Rogue in the Blamey Stakes. Bart was also reported in the press as having said, 'Breaking Amiable's record is a feat that not many would have thought possible.'

Bart's fellow champion trainer Geoff Murphy added, 'I told the bloke next to me that this horse has gone too hard when it reached the 400 metres but hell, he accelerated again and again. He's incredible.' (*The Sunday Mail* 14 February 1988.)

Vic explained, 'He is not out to run records, he just does that himself.'

Cyril's response was simple: 'There is still improvement in Vo Rogue.'

Les Carlyon, writing for *The Sydney Morning Herald* on 15 February, put Vo's Blamey Stakes win into perspective:

> Amiable ran the equivalent of 1min 34.2s back in 1940. That was two generations ago, before Dunkirk, before Pearl Harbour, and five years before Victory Robert Rail was born. Amiable was absolutely flat to beat two classy ones—High Caste and Ajax, no less—in the C.M. Lloyd Stakes. The record seemed set in stone.
>
> Vo Rogue merely flicked the ground, enjoying himself and posted 1min 34s dead. He was never flat. As Cyril Small put it: 'He could have run a bit faster time.' Small delivered the line deadpan, without the hint of a boast. It was easy to believe him. Quite simply, Vo Rogue is the best front runner in memory.

By now, the trainers were trying to work out how on earth they could possibly beat this horse. Many of Vo's equine opposition had regal blood running through their veins, their trainers had collectively won pretty much all the best races in the country, and their jockeys could arguably take their places amongst the best in the world. Yet, when Vo Rogue, Vic Rail and Cyril Small turned up to compete against them on a hard racing surface, all they could do was follow and watch Vo and Cyril disappear from sight at sustained speed. But the Colin Hayes camp hatched a plan for the St George Stakes to bring Vo undone and put a stop to his dominance.

While the plot to bring Vo undone was being devised, in the background, a minor change was going on with the ownership of Vo.

It was no secret that John Murray, who took a back seat in the management of Vo, had his 20 per cent share up for sale. There was talk at one stage that the new part-owner might be Bert Newton. That was exciting. Who didn't love Moonface? He was as much a part of Australian television as, well, Australian television. His skits with Graham Kennedy and Don Lane still bring the house down to this very day. But Bert didn't buy into the horse. Instead, a fellow called Garry Roberts did.

* * *

Garry was and still is a Melbourne boy through and through. Tall and thin with light brown hair, Garry grew up in Moonee Ponds and left school at the age of 14 due to his poor eyesight. Garry is legally blind when it comes to small print, needing to magnify it to read it. His eyesight is better looking into the distance, but he still can't see clearly. Despite sitting in the front row at school, Garry couldn't read the words on the blackboard and he got to the point where he couldn't handle school anymore. His parents agreed that he could leave and get a job. By the time he turned 20, Garry knew that he wanted to be a professional punter, and that's what he became. Garry has been involved in other aspects of racing including working as a bloodstock agent. He is also revered as an astute form analyst.

Garry was mates with racing journalist Shane Templeton who took a keen interest in Vo. Shane would ring Vic and Jeff regularly and it was from Shane that Garry—who was a big fan of the horse—became aware that a 20 per cent share in Vo was for sale. It didn't come cheaply though. The price tag was $180,000 which valued Vo at $900,000—a massive amount for a gelding who had no residual value after racing. Should the horse have suffered any injury that would reduce his performance or bring his racing career to a halt, Garry would have done his dough. It was a huge risk to take.

As Garry was a professional punter, the popular theory was that Garry had won the money backing Vo, but Garry tells me that certainly was not correct.

'That's not right,' Garry states. 'I might have been winning some money during the races at the time, but I borrowed the money against the property, I took out a second mortgage on the house at Templestowe.'

It should be remembered that back in 1988, home loan rates were around 13.5 to 14 per cent. I ask Garry what his wife thought about him taking out a second mortgage on the house to buy a share in a gelded racehorse.

'Well, she said, "As long as you think you know what you're doing." I said I hope so, but I'll take the risk. I'm a gambler so I'll take the risk. And it worked out okay in the end.'

Indeed it did.

On 23 February 1988, Garry Roberts officially became the newest addition to Team Vo and climbed on board for the ride of a lifetime.

Garry didn't have to wait too long to see a return on his investment. Just four days after signing the ownership papers, Garry was on course at Caulfield to cheer on his horse. Of the five runners to face the starter in the St George Stakes, Colin Hayes trained two of them: Cossack Warrior, ridden by stable jockey Michael Clarke and Dowie, the outsider of the field at 50/1 ($51) ridden by Michael's brother Gary.

As the field jumped, the Hayes camp put their plan into practice and Dowie challenged Vo for the lead. Rather than being left to run along on his own, Vo would have company. Dowie's jockey was roaring at his horse, Cyril thinks in an attempt to unsettle Vo and fire him up. Cyril caught on quickly to the plan and wasn't about to get caught in a head-to-head battle with any horse, let alone the outsider.

Cyril eased Vo to allow Dowie to take up the running. Vo sat comfortably behind him in second place. As the field turned for home Vo had the better of Dowie who was fading badly. Cossack Warrior raced up to Vo's girth but his efforts were short-lived as Vo bounded away from him to win the race comfortably by three lengths.

The team riding tactics that would be discussed in the press and everywhere else but the stewards' room, were not lost on race caller Bill Collins who exclaimed, 'Vo Rogue's gonna do it again, you can't beat him no matter what you do.' The 1/5 ($1.20) favourite smashed the previous track record for 1800 metres by an incredible 1.5 seconds, running 1-47.30 on a track rated a Firm 2. As Garry Roberts said to me, 'That's nine lengths, no horse does that anymore.' Dowie finished last of the five runners, some 28 lengths behind Vo. A very proud Garry Roberts led Vo and Cyril back to scale to the cheers of the crowd.

Futurity Stakes

The headline in *The Sporting Australian* written by Graeme Kelly on 29 February 1988 read: 'Futurity, not Bonecrusher, Vo Rogue's big danger'. In time, the headline would prove to be correct, but not for the reasons Mr Kelly wrote about. The article discussed the potential for Vo to be beaten that preparation in the Futurity Stakes. Time would tell that the Futurity Stakes would ultimately beat Vo Rogue.

With Jeff still in Brisbane, his friend who was helping Vic with Vo called Jeff and suggested he come back to Melbourne as soon as he could. His friend told Jeff that Vic wasn't training Vo for the 2000 metres of the Australian Cup, he had changed his training routine toward the Futurity, a sprint race. Jeff called Vic and asked him what he was doing. Vic replied that the horse would go to the Futurity Stakes. Jeff explained that the Futurity really wasn't the race they were targeting—Jeff wanted the Australian Cup. Vic replied that Vo would 'just pick up the Futurity Stakes on the way through'. And so, the Futurity Stakes was confirmed in the schedule. Jeff returned to Melbourne in the week leading into the race.

On Futurity Stakes race day, more than 100 people stood around Vo's horse stall as he was being saddled for the race. Also, there was a *60 Minutes* crew shooting film for an upcoming episode.

The Futurity Stakes field was a good one that included up and coming three-year-old Rancho Ruler, sprinter Cameronic, King Phoenix who was runner up to Rubiton the previous year, and Campaign King, a brilliant sprinter-miler and the obvious danger to Vo. Campaign King was already the winner of multiple Group 1 WFA events including the William Reid and Futurity Stakes in 1986, and the George Ryder, All Aged Stakes and George Main Stakes in 1987. Bart Cummings trained Campaign King who was ridden by Harry White. Bart's philosophy was that Rancho Ruler might break up Vo, allowing Campaign King to chase him and pass him. It was Bart's view that he wouldn't be surprised to see his horse win handsomely.

When the field jumped, Vo took up his customary position at the front of the field. Rancho Ruler was left to do the chasing while Harry had Campaign King tucked away in fourth place on the fence. Coming into the straight Campaign King was about three lengths behind Vo but very quickly reduced that margin to a length, then a half-length. At the 200-metre mark, it appeared that Campaign King was travelling better than Vo and might just beat him after all.

I was watching the race in the Guineas Room at Eagle Farm racecourse with Lorraine McLachlan, wife of Queensland's champion trainer Bruce, and a group of other ladies. I was cheering for Vo and

Cyril but conceded Vo may have met his match. But Vo was never a quitter and responded to the challenge.

As the field flew past the winning post Lorraine said to me, 'He's got it, he's won.' Vo fought off Campaign King to win by a head.

Harry later said that he thought Campaign King would beat Vo for sure but Vo found another half-length and Campaign King struggled. Tony Bourke, writing for *The Age* newspaper, wrote that Harry suggested had the race been a further 50 metres, Vo would have won by a further margin. Clem Dimsey reporting for the *Sunday Telegraph* quoted Harry telling those around him after the race that, 'I think the only way to stop him would be with a sledgehammer.'

Vo ran a new track record of 1-22.2, taking .02 off the previous record set by Galleon six years earlier. Some sections of the crowd were still clapping Vo 20 minutes after the race. The crowd stood 10-deep around the mounting yard listening to the presentation hosted by Sir Rupert Clarke, then Chairman of the Victoria Amateur Turf Club. In his speech, Sir Rupert mentioned Vo in the same sentence as three immortals of the turf: Phar Lap, Ajax and Bernborough.

While most media and the general public were searching for superlatives not previously used to describe Vo's scintillating victory, Les Carlyon, writing for *The Sydney Morning Herald*, made what was to be a critical observation. In that newspaper published the following Monday, Mr Carlyon wrote,

> Vo Rogue was awesome, but it was a hard run. The gelding blew badly on return to scale, was soaked in sweat from shoulder to rump, and tucked up for about ten minutes or so.

It would be less than two weeks before the true extent of those observations would be revealed.

Soon after the Futurity, Tommy Smith contacted Jeff and offered to train Vo for free, telling Jeff that he would improve Vo. Jeff laughed at him and asked Tommy to explain how he would improve a horse that had broken three track records in a row.

CHAPTER 7

THE MATCH RACE OF THE CENTURY

The Bicentenary Australian Cup was billed as the 'Match Race of the Century', and despite a field of eight runners, the public was only interested in two of them: Australia's newest champion Vo Rogue and New Zealand's champion Bonecrusher, ridden for the majority of his career by Gary Stewart. The marvellous thing about these two great champions, and one of the many reasons I think they were so dearly adored by the racing public, is that their purchase prices were humble four figure amounts. Vo was purchased privately as a weanling for a sum that would value him at $5000, and Bonecrusher was purchased at the Waikato Yearling Sales by Peter Mitchell for NZ$3250.

Meanwhile, the Colin Hayes-trained Authaal that was lining up alongside them was owned by Sheikh Mohammed bin Rashid Al Maktoum. He was reportedly purchased as a yearling from the Goffs sale in Dublin for the equivalent of AUD$7.3 million—an extraordinary amount of money for a horse at that time, and still is today, and inconceivable for the average Joe. He was as regally-bred as any horse racing anywhere in the world. He was by Shergar out of a Nijinsky mare. Shergar was a champion racehorse and the Epsom

Derby, Irish Derby, King George VI Stakes and Queen Elizabeth Stakes represent a few of his major victories. He was owned by the Aga Khan who later syndicated him and retired him to stud in Ireland. The Aga Khan retained a 15 per cent share in the prize stallion. Shergar was famously kidnapped in February of 1983—reportedly by the IRA—and held for ransom. The ransom was never paid and Shergar was never recovered. Aside from his breeding, Authaal's claim to fame was winning the Group 1 Irish St Ledger prior to coming to Australia.

Bonecrusher or 'Big Red' as he was affectionately known by those closest to him, had taken all before him having won numerous Group 1 events as a three-year-old including the New Zealand Derby (1985), Air New Zealand Stakes (1986), Australian Derby (1986) and Tancred Stakes (1986).

In his four-year-old season he did not disappoint his growing legion of fans and built upon his extensive and highly impressive resume by adding to it Group 1 races including the Underwood Stakes (1986), Caulfield Stakes (1986), the WS Cox Plate (1986) and the Australian Cup (1987). His Cox Plate win defeating rival champion New Zealand horse Our Waverley Star continues to be one of the most talked about and replayed races in modern racing history. The horses took off almost in unison, raced away from the rest of the field at the 600-metre mark, and had a titanic head-to-head battle all the way to the winning post. Bonecrusher edged to a narrow margin in the shadows of the post to gain victory. Race caller Bill Collins declared, 'Bonecrusher races into equine immortality.' The battle was fierce and relentless. Both horses showed extraordinary courage and while there was only one winner, both horses became Australasian heroes on that day. It is not often that people remember who ran second in any race.

After his win in the 1987 Australian Cup, Bonecrusher ran third in the Group 1 Rawson Stakes over 2000 metres at Rosehill on 28 March. On that occasion he was ridden by champion Sydney-based jockey Shane Dye. He didn't race again until 13 February 1988 when he opened his five-year-old season in New Zealand, winning the Group 3

White Robe at Wingatui over 1600 metres. That was the same day Vo broke the track record at Flemington in winning the Blamey Stakes, also over 1600 metres. Two weeks later on 27 February, Bonecrusher won the Group 1 Air New Zealand Stakes over 2000 metres at Ellerslie for the second time, the same day Vo won the St George Stakes smashing the previous track record.

While Vo had to contend with team riding to win the St George Stakes, Bonecrusher had his own problems to overcome in winning the Air New Zealand. He missed the start and was blocked for a run in the straight. But as his trainer Frank Ritchie told the press reporting for *The Australian* newspaper, 'Nobody told him he couldn't win', and as all champions do, Bonecrusher found that extra something that got him over the line.

Interestingly, the Auckland Racing Club (ARC) contacted Jeff and Vic a week prior and invited them to run in the Air New Zealand Stakes. The ARC offered to fly Vo over for a match race of their own. However, the very short notice, along with the preferred option of an 1800 metres race at that time of Vo's preparation rather than a 2000 metres race, saw the Team remain in Melbourne.

Back in New Zealand, so impressive was Bonecrusher's performance it prompted journalist Bruce Clark, who was based in Brisbane at the time and writing for *The Courier Mail* and *The Sunday Mail*, to declare in his Sunday write-up on 28 February 1988, 'Forget Rogue!'

Bonecrusher's owner Peter Mitchell was quoted in *The Australian* newspaper on 29 February as having said, 'Tell Vo Rogue's jockey to fill his saddle bags with grenades and drop them behind him up the Flemington straight … because that's the only way he is going to stop 'Red' coming at him.'

But Mr Mitchell and the Bonecrusher camp had a looming obstacle to navigate through that was more worrisome than grenades being dropped in front of their great horse. The airline the horse was booked on to fly him from Auckland into Melbourne was cancelled due to cyclonic weather. Bonecrusher was stranded in Auckland and unlikely to make the race. The news sent shock waves through the Victoria Racing Club (VRC) offices. The Club had spent significant amounts of money promoting the clash of the two superstars. News reports claimed that the VRC was catering for a crowd of 35,000. With Bonecrusher a potential no-show, there was a risk that the crowd numbers could drop to less than half that. Further, there was the obvious disappointment to consider that would be felt by the racing community and general public, who had been counting down the weeks and days to the race.

Every possible effort was made by the VRC to bring Bonecrusher safely to Melbourne. It was reported in some sections of the media that the VRC chartered an Ansett freighter at a cost of around $40,000. And if so, good on them for doing that. It was the right thing to do for the good of racing. There was the usual bitching by some about showing favouritism etcetera, but regardless of how much it cost them if the VRC did pay the bill, it was money well spent.

The Air New Zealand Stakes was Bonecrusher's last race before competing in the Bicentenary Australian Cup. He would go into the Cup with just two runs under his belt and coming off the back of an 11-month break.

Vo on the other hand had five runs under his belt, was unbeaten in the current campaign, and was breaking track records left, right and centre.

Tommy Smith had reportedly declared Vo the best horse in the world up to 2000 metres. Much had been said and much more had been written about Vo Rogue, Bonecrusher and the 'Match Race of the Century', the 1988 Bicentenary Australian Cup. Actions speak louder than any words and there was only one way this battle was going to be decided, and that was on the track.

Jeff summed it up best when he said, 'I'm glad Bonecrusher has come back for his owner and his trainer Frank Ritchie. But as far as we are concerned, let the best horse win the Australian Cup, whether it be Vo Rogue, Bonecrusher or something else.'

* * *

As we were packing on the Saturday afternoon to head down to Melbourne the very next morning, Cyril asked me to iron his jockey breeches. These were the very same breeches he had worn to victory in the five races preceding the Australian Cup. I called them the lucky breeches. In a hurry I didn't turn the heat down on the iron and burned a hole right through them. 'Oh God no, I've burned the lucky breeches!' I screamed out in horror.

My mother was visiting, and she said, 'It's all right, I'll patch them with a hanky.'

'It's not all right', I said. 'I've destroyed them. The horse won't win now. He can't win if Cyril isn't wearing the lucky breeches.' I was completely distraught and inconsolable.

Cyril, being the level-headed and measured person that he is wasn't overly worried about it. He went to his gear room, pulled out another pair and packed them instead.

We flew into Tullamarine on the Sunday morning; the race was on the Monday. Jeff greeted us and as he always does, he got straight to the point. 'The horse can't win. He's not right. He hasn't recovered from the Futurity Stakes run. If the race was run yesterday I would have scratched him. He'll run nearer last than first!'

Bloody hell! What do you say to that? In typical Cyril style, he said nothing and continued listening as Jeff spoke. My head was spinning thinking of Cyril. The very next day he would be riding in a race deemed the 'Match Race of the Century' on a horse dearly loved by the nation's racing public and who was the even money favourite up against the New Zealand champion. The owner, who knew Vo better than anyone else, has declared the horse can't win. Jeff went on to say that the horse was flat and had only just started picking himself up. By the following Saturday, Vo would have been right. But the race wasn't six days away, it was one day. It was one of those times when we had to hope for the best while expecting the worst.

On our way to our accommodation, we stopped in at the Queen Victoria Market to have a look around. We all wanted ice cream, although after Jeff's news, a stiff drink was probably a better choice. Cyril and I went into the ice cream shop and Jeff waited outside.

The Greek man serving us said to Cyril, 'Has anyone ever told you that you look like Cyril Small?'

Cyril looked blankly at him and the man continued, 'You know, Cyril Small, he rides Vo Rogue.'

Cyril nodded in acknowledgement that he knew who he was talking about.

'Me and Cyril, we're like this', said the man as he crossed his fingers to suggest they had a tight friendship. 'We were out on the town together last night,' the man continued.

'Oh good,' said Cyril as he took the ice creams and we walked out of the shop. We told Jeff about the brief conversation and we all had a laugh wondering one of two things: was that nice Greek man having us on, or was there a person in Melbourne who looked like Cyril who was having him on? It really didn't matter. We had a destroyed pair of lucky breeches and a jaded even money favourite for the 'Match Race of the Century' to worry about. Welcome to Melbourne!

* * *

As Jeff, Vic, Cyril and I walked into Flemington, the atmosphere was electric. Some likened it to a footy grand final. I've never been to a footy grand final so I wouldn't know about that. But for sure and certain, the punters had picked their team. Those supporting Bonecrusher wore blue 'C'mon Crusher' badges and those supporting Vo, including me, wore red 'Go Rogue Go' badges.

An hour or so later, crowds stood around the tie-up stalls of both champions as they were being saddled. Some of the dads in the crowd put their young kids on their shoulders so they had a better chance of seeing the star horses. The crowds followed Vo and Bonecrusher to the parade yard and as the two A-listers walked down the long Flemington walkway and onto the track, the people clapped and cheered their heroes.

Channel Ten broadcasted the Australian Cup with outstanding sports broadcaster Bruce McAvaney as their race caller. To relive this incredible moment in Australian racing history, I suggest you go onto YouTube. But for now, I have transcribed the telecast, in part, for you. As the horses paraded behind the barriers Brue McAvaney set the scene, telling the viewers:

> There is a magnificent crowd at this famous Flemington course, and they cheered when Bonecrusher and Vo Rogue came out onto the track. Vo Rogue is still favourite with bookmakers, Bonecrusher has been a steady second favourite, and there's been good money for Cossack Warrior and Authaal. Authaal cost $7.3 million as a yearling, Bonecrusher cost $3200 and Vo Rogue at eleven months of age cost $5000. Authaal is owned by the richest and most successful owner in racing, Sheikh Mohammad, Cossack Warrior by the famous Robert Sangster, and Vo Rogue and Bonecrusher—well, they're owned by battlers in comparison.

I sat in the grandstand with knots in my stomach. When the gates opened Vo went straight to the lead. From that moment to coming into the home turn, Vo was anywhere between four and seven lengths in front of Authaal and Bonecrusher. Well into the home straight and the crowd of nearly 34,000 people were on their feet and roaring, mostly for Vo as Bonecrusher was not making any ground on the Australian champion. Halfway down the straight Vo was a 'mile' in front. All on track and those watching on TV screens across Australia expected another outstanding win. I was screaming out encouragement to Cyril and Vo. I was so sure Jeff had got it wrong. There was no possible way Vo could be beaten.

Back on Channel Ten and Bruce McAvaney's voice was roaring

with as much excitement as the crowd, and he called:

> Three hundred to go, they're not going to get this superstar. Vo Rogue's about eight lengths in front of Dandy Andy, Bonecrusher can't get to him and Bahrain. At the distance Dandy Andy's running on, Vo Rogue's four in front. Dandy Andy's getting to him. Vo Rogue's two in front, Dandy Andy's flying, he will get him. Here's a boilover in the Cup, Dandy Andy and Brent Thomspon's got up to beat Vo Rogue, third Bonecrusher, Bahrain, Island Spy, Cossack Warrior, Authaal and King of Brooklyn.

For their legions of fans, the unthinkable had happened.

Vo had been beaten, and so had Bonecrusher. Not just a little bit though. With Vo stopping and Dandy Andy finishing strongly, Dandy Andy moved away to win the race by one and a half lengths to Vo, with Bonecrusher a further five lengths behind Vo in third place. People in the crowd could be heard booing as the horses were pulling up.

To his fans and everyone else not connected to the horse, Vo had been beaten in a boil over. The 'Match Race of the Century' had been hijacked by the 125/1 ($126) outsider. But in fact, Vo had run out of his skin. He gave everything he had plus some, but on that day it just wasn't enough. He didn't run nearer last than first though as Jeff had suggested only a day earlier.

Post-race Bruce McAvaney had this to say:

> Well Vo Rogue, I said he was home the super horse and if I saw it again I'd say it again, because he was eight lengths in front and he was flying in front, but here's Dandy Andy and about now you can see there is a little danger [200-metre mark]. Bonecrusher was beaten, Big Red could do no more. Bahrain was in front of him, and Vo Rogue, Small has had to produce everything here—Dandy Andy's flying, Vo Rogue's paddling and the impossible has happened. Vo Rogue's been picked up by Dandy Andy, he's gone straight past him, Brent

Thompson. Vo Rogue who's a great fighter could find no more today, and Dandy Andy has gone on to win the Australian Cup, Vo Rogue second.

Over on radio 3UZ race caller Bill Collins when summing up the result proclaimed the now famous words, 'Goodness gracious me.'

With the large crowd in disbelief and many still booing, Dandy Andy's jockey 'The Babe' Brent Thompson, who only minutes earlier commented that he would rather be in the stand watching the race than riding in it, brought the horse back to scale. Brent had initially knocked back the ride on Dandy Andy in preference to watching the race from the grandstand, but the trainer put him on at acceptance time anyway.

As the cameramen lined up to take his photo, Dandy Andy's trainer from country Victoria, 76-year-old Jim Cerchi and father of 13, pulled out a piece of paper from his coat jacket and scribbled on it, 'Come on Dandy Andy'. The press gathered around Jeff wanting his thoughts. 'He's been beaten by a better horse on the day,' said Jeff. And that he had. Dandy Andy as Jeff rightly points out to this day, was no slouch. He had won the Group 1 Doomben Cup over 2000 metres in WFA conditions only 10 months earlier.

And so it came to pass that the best horse on that day won the Australian Cup. It wasn't Vo Rogue and it wasn't Bonecrusher, it was 'something else'.

Mr Cerchi was quoted in *The Age* newspaper on 26 February as having said, 'I think Vo Rogue is the best 'miler' since Ajax, but they can all be beaten'. To this day, the 1988 Australian Cup win by Dandy Andy is considered one of the biggest boilovers in Australian racing history.

* * *

Sometime long after the race, I was sitting on my own waiting for Cyril to leave the jockeys' room and head on back to our accommodation, or back to the stables to see Vo. At that time, Rod Johnson was the CEO of the VRC. I remember him as being a lovely man, a gentleman in fact. Rod came over to me and invited me to go with him to the Committee Room for a drink. I thanked him but declined the invitation. 'I am waiting for my husband,' I said to him.

'Yes I know, he can come too,' he replied.

'But he's a jockey,' I responded.

'I know who he is,' said Rod. 'And he knows his way there. You come with me.'

To provide context around that conversation, at that time in Queensland, jockeys were not permitted in the members stand or lounges, let alone the Committee Room, by order of the then Queensland Turf Club that ran racing in Queensland. At least, that was the situation at the city tracks, Eagle Farm and Doomben. I don't really know why that was. I always thought it was a very ordinary decision, particularly as the jockeys risked their lives putting on the show all day long while the committee persons and members enjoyed said show from the safety of relatively lavish surrounds. One would have thought that the jockeys had earned the right to have a drink and relax in the members lounges after a hard day at the office. The rules did eventually change though—they had to. Jockeys are now welcome pretty much everywhere on course, except in the betting ring.

As I walked with Rod to the Committee Room I found myself lost in the extraordinary history of racing in Victoria. Rod went inside but I remained behind for a few moments, looking at the trophies, reading the plaques and embracing the memorabilia. I could have stayed there for hours. It was a museum and I felt so privileged to be there. As I moved towards the door of the Committee Room I could see it was a who's who of racing inside. There were numerous high-profile jockeys and trainers who I instantly recognised but had never met. Jeff had settled in and was in conversation with the Bonecrusher camp.

There was also some banter between Jeff and a member of the press who had appointed himself as the unofficial president of the Vo

Rogue fan club. He was keen to tell people that he was advising the Vo Rogue camp during the campaign. Jeff called to him from across the room, 'We're taking the blinkers off that horse next campaign, is that your idea too?'

I couldn't help but smile. Nobody advised the Vo Rogue camp but Jeff himself. Jeff was in charge; he ran the show.

In fact, after the Futurity Stakes, Tony Bourke of *The Age* newspaper wrote of Jeff, 'Perry gives the impression of a man not to be argued with.' He was right about that. The blinkers didn't come off next prep—that gear change was delayed.

Meanwhile, Vic was to the side of the room surrounded by beautifully-dressed and manicured mature-age ladies who listened attentively to every word he spoke. They appeared captivated by him and somewhat curious. I assumed these ladies were the wives of the committeemen and other stakeholders. Vic loved nothing more than having a yarn, and as the trainer of Vo Rogue, he was never short on conversation or lacking an audience. Vic wasn't loud, nor was he arrogant. He was humble and entertaining, and he certainly did not disappoint those who gathered around him to listen to what he had to say.

Cyril arrived as Rod assured me he would. I was just as much awestruck as I was excited by the event and happy Cyril was now by my side. We joined Jeff in conversation with Bonecrusher's connections. They were lovely down-to-earth people. Neither camp got the result they had hoped for, but everyone was proud of their horses and accepting of the fact they were beaten fair and square by one better on the day—the horse that to this day I lovingly refer to as Dandy Bloody Andy. If anyone was going to upstage the stars that day, I'm so glad it was him.

* * *

Tony Meany reporting for *The Sun* newspaper the day after the Australian Cup led with the headline, 'Bo, Vo over-rated' and went on to say, 'BONECRUSHER and Vo Rogue are grossly over-rated …

Neither Vo Rogue nor Bonecrusher has beaten champion horses. And they never will.'

I never particularly warmed to Tony Meany's style of journalism. I found it to be quite abrupt and sometimes offensive. I've learned though in racing, in order to survive you have to toughen up and be less emotive when reading stories in the press, and now of course on social media, which Cyril and I stay away from.

Tony Bourke on the other hand, reporting for *The Age* newspaper, gave a more considered summation of the Australian Cup result and suggested that Vo's defeat may have been due to the track being softer than Vo liked it. Mr Bourke also lamented that, 'Maybe his hard run to win the Futurity Stakes (1400 metres) at Caulfield only 10 days ago took more out of him than we thought.'

A few days after the Australian Cup, Jeff was concerned about Vo and called the VRC vet to examine him and take a heart score of the horse. The vet found that Vo had strained his heart. Tony Bourke was correct. 'The horse tried that hard in the Futurity,' said Jeff.

As it turned out, Graeme Kelly's headline a few weeks earlier also proved to be correct. It was the Futurity and not Bonecrusher that was Vo's big danger. But it was Les Carlyon's powers of observation that were spot on as he had stated after the Futurity that, 'The gelding blew badly on return to scale, was soaked in sweat from shoulder to rump, and tucked up for about 10 minutes or so.'

The vet told Jeff that Vo would have to have three months off from racing. Jeff was furious with Vic. Jeff blamed Vic for Vo's condition, for not sticking to the plan and for changing Vo's training regime. The trip back to Brisbane was not a good one. The two had an altercation in the car on the way home, with Jeff telling Vic that he didn't deserve the horse. Jeff said that he had seen the best trainers with top line horses try to win the Doomben 10,000 over 1350 metres and a week later step them up to the 2020 metres of the Doomben Cup.

'They just raced exactly the same way as Vo did,' Jeff recalls. 'Go to win and then die in the last 100 yards. They'd run a good race, run second or third and you know they'd get beaten because, and even the good trainers in Brisbane would tell you, you can't take them from a seven-furlong (1400 metres) race to ten furlongs (2000 metres) in a week. And I tell you that they were all right, and that's what I said to Vicky.'

With the horse in the spelling yard Jeff was contemplating the horse's future, and that of his trainer. A young Brisbane trainer had started to make some inroads among the Brisbane training ranks with his small team. Jeff, still angry with Vic over Vo's strained heart, was considering switching the horse to him. Jeff saw the young trainer as a good fit with the Team. However, after some soul searching and a lengthy discussion with Vic, followed by a stern warning, Vo returned to Vic's stable.

'He knew he'd done wrong,' Jeff says of Vic. 'He knew he'd fucked up, that's what it amounted to.'

* * *

While all that was going on, Cyril returned to Queensland. On the Saturday following the Australian Cup, he won the $250,000 Golden Nugget Stakes for two-year-olds on Ancaro at the Gold Coast for trainer Merv Lewis. In fact, he rode a treble that day and backed up three days later with a winner at Ipswich. He took a break for most of April and then rode 16 winners across May and June. At the end of July, Vo returned to racing and was crowned Queensland Horse of the Year for the 1987/88 racing year.

Jeff, Cyril and Vic attended the racing awards which was a day-time event. Vic was a non-drinker, Cyril and Jeff are not.

Clearly Cyril and Jeff had a fabulous time. Cyril brought Jeff home with him to our place at Hendra. Our house had a very steep internal timber staircase leading to the upstairs living areas. I stood at the top of those stairs and watched on in horror as Jeff made his way up them with Cyril pushing him from behind, trying to keep him balanced. It was like watching a pebble pushing a boulder up a hill. Both of them were very unsteady on their feet, particularly Jeff. As they got to the top of the stairs Jeff made his way toward the lounge, only to stumble and fall into the fixed glass windowpane of the large set of sliding glass doors that led to the balcony. The windows shook like a monster wobble board and Jeff fell into the lounge safe and sound, nothing broken, no harm done. The end result was definitely all about good luck rather than good management.

The woman behind Team Vo

There's an old saying, 'Behind every great man is a great woman', and the woman behind Team Vo was Debby Osborne.

With Vic interstate with Vo for months at a time, and on multiple occasions across the years, he needed a reliable, capable, trustworthy, and resilient person to take care of business. To the general public, Debby was out of view to the point of being invisible. But the fact is, Vic's racing operation would never have held together without her.

'Debby was the backbone of the operation,' Jeff says. 'Debby's role in Vo's development and career, and the subsequent management of Vic's stables when he went interstate should never be underestimated.'

For a very long time, and particularly when Vo was racing, I had no understanding about what was involved in running a racing stable, and I never gave Debby's workload any thought at all. Many years on and now having a trainer's licence of my own, and having bred, purchased and trained racehorses, I am acutely aware of what is involved. Today I have a real appreciation for Debby's work ethic and the enormity of her achievements during those times. On reflection, Debby's efforts on a day-to-day basis were nothing less than herculean. From my experience, there is rarely a day at the stable when a horse isn't sick, injured, shifted a plate, hasn't eaten or, well, the list goes on.

Vic had anywhere between 14 and 22 horses in work in Brisbane when he took horses interstate and left Debby in charge. For a while, Debby had Vic's son Troy living with them and Troy would help out, but it was Debby who bore the brunt of the work. It is significant to remember that at that time, Debby was a young woman in her mid-20s when she held that responsibility.

I asked Debby how she managed that extraordinary workload on a daily basis that included getting anywhere between 14 to 22 horses, that were housed across multiple properties, fed and watered, and their stables cleaned each morning and afternoon, getting the horses to the track to work them before closing time which was 8.00am (she rode them trackwork as well), attending to their health and welfare issues, and on race day, getting them to the races and often also being their jockey.

Debby gave me a simple answer. She told me, 'You just keep working. You've got to feed them, you've got to water them, you've got to clean their boxes. I used to get up at 2.30 in the morning and start at 3am. You get up and work until the work's done.'

On race day, in Vic's absence, and because Debby held a jockey's licence and was still actively race riding, Vic had to obtain special permission from the stewards officiating at country meetings for Debby to saddle up. Permission was granted on the condition that Debby was not riding the horses. On days that Debby was riding Vic's horses, another trainer was appointed to deputise for Vic. Debby would take the horse or horses to the meeting and provide the stewards with a letter advising the trainer who was in charge of the horse or horses on race day. If the meeting was at Doomben or Eagle Farm, Debby was allowed to saddle up because she was not licensed to ride at city meetings.

Added to that workload, in 1988, Debby and Vic moved into their new racing complex, Victory Lodge at 12 Williams Avenue in Hendra. Debby did a great deal to set up house for them there as well. Vic told Alan Welburn who interviewed him for the *Sunday Mail* magazine published on 23 July 1989, 'Without Debby on my side I'd be lost. I probably would have gone down the gurgler years ago. But she has stuck like glue.' Debby epitomises my theory that anyone who is allergic to work need not apply for a job working in a racing stable.

CHAPTER 8

THE SPRING OF '88

With the Brisbane stable in great hands, the Team first headed to Sydney. Vo's spring campaign of '88 got off to a very slow start. He finished down the track in the Missile Stakes at Rosehill on a Good 3 track. Vo was stabled at Kembla Grange and the Club asked if Vo could do an exhibition gallop between races at their Saturday meeting the week following his Missile Stakes run.

Jeff and Vic were keen for Cyril to come down and ride Vo, however, the Club arranged for another jockey riding at the meeting on the day to take him around. The exhibition gallop was meant to be more like a trackwork exercise with a three-quarter gallop over 400 metres to the line. The following Saturday he was lining up in the Premiere Stakes, also at Rosehill, so they didn't want Vo knocked around. The jockey couldn't hold Vo in the exhibition gallop and he bolted on him. The edge was taken off Vo and it took Vic about four weeks to get the horse right again. Subsequently, he finished down the track in the Premiere Stakes.

Team Vo then headed to Melbourne where they continued their run of outs. Vo beat just one horse home in the Manikato Stakes at

Moonee Valley on a Soft 5 track and again finished down the track in the Craiglee Stakes at Flemington on a Good 3 track. Finally, at his fifth start, Vo returned to some form which coincided with him racing on a Firm 2 track. Vo ran a promising third behind Our Poetic Prince and Flotilla in the John F Feehan Stakes at Moonee Valley, a race he had finished second in the year before behind Rubiton.

The Team was confident Vo's third placing was a true sign that he was on track now for the rest of the spring. His acid test would be his next start, the Turnbull Stakes, a race he had won the year before when he bravely defeated Fair Sir.

On the morning of the Turnbull Stakes, *The Age* newspaper published an article written by Cathy Walker that captured Vic's outlook at that time quite well. The article stated, 'trainer Vic Rail, whose colourful personality has faded to muted shades since Vo Rogue's shaky start to his spring campaign, said yesterday he believed Vo Rogue "was just about right now" …'

The punters thought so too, and Vo started favourite at 7/4 to win back-to-back Turnbulls. The only threat the public could see to him was Fair Sir who started at 3/1 ($4). As it turned out, there was no threat to him. Vo trounced the opposition and had two lengths to spare to Apollo Run and Ebeli Show. Fair Sir didn't fire a shot and finished 10 lengths behind him. Fair Sir was retired to stud duties three weeks later after finishing down the track in his subsequent three races.

* * *

On many occasions I suggested to Cyril that he should not take any other rides outside of Vo when Vo was racing, reasoning that it just wasn't worth it. Back then the losing riding fee was $50. The jockey's percentage of five per cent of the prizemoney Vo was racing for was substantially more than that. This was a once in a lifetime opportunity and all risks should be minimised. Cyril didn't subscribe fully to my theory, although he was selective in what rides he did take.

But then the day arrived, four days after winning the Turnbull Stakes, that Cyril was suspended for careless riding on another horse, Kenesta, at Doomben. He caused interference to a horse our good friend Neil Williams was riding and while Cyril pleaded to the stewards to fine him rather than suspend him, their answer was 'No'.

Vo was all set to run in the Group 1 Caulfield Stakes (WFA) over 2000 metres on the Saturday. With Cyril suspended, Jeff and Vic were left to find a new jockey to wear the now famous brown jacket with white hooped sleeves and white cap. However, after some careful thought they decided to scratch Vo from the event. Jeff didn't want to run Vo four times over 2000 metres in the space of a month and Cyril's suspension sealed the deal, making the decision to scratch an easy one. The problem was only solved for one week though because the Team wanted Vo to have one more run as a pipe opener before the WS Cox Plate. There was one suitable race for him: the Richard Ellis Plate over 1400 metres at Caulfield on 15 October 1988. Cyril was still suspended on that day so the search was on for a replacement jockey.

The search came to an end when trainer John Poletti suggested to Vic that he engage champion jockey Peter Cook for the ride. The son of jockey Billy Cook—also a noted champion of the pigskin—Peter emulated his father's dual Melbourne Cup winning successes by winning two Melbourne Cups himself, the first on Just A Dash (1981) and the second on Black Knight (1984). Peter also had two Cox Plate wins to his name courtesy of champion filly Surround (1976) and my favourite, 'The King' Kingston Town (1982). Coincidently, Peter also substituted for The King's usual jockey Malcolm Johnston who also happened to be suspended for that Cox Plate win. Peter had enormous talent and great hands, and his resume extended far beyond those illustrious wins. It's fair to say he was no stranger to riding a champion.

Peter recalls riding trackwork at Flemington for John Poletti and Bart Cummings when Vic came looking for a substitute rider. 'Vic was talking with John Poletti. John said to him "Peter Cook's over there, go and ask him,"' Peter says. 'Vic came and asked me, and I said yeah, good as gold. Vic said he would check with Jeff, and he later confirmed with me that I could ride the horse.'

As the race was a handicap event, Vo carried 61kg. He drew barrier 13 in a field of 16. There was no expectation by Vic or Jeff that Vo would win the race. He was merely there to keep his fitness in check in readiness for the Cox Plate. In fact, Ron Maund writing for *The Sportman* on the Friday before the race stated, 'Naturally Vo Rogue will be flat out to win tomorrow.' His legion of fans didn't think so and Vo went to the barriers as the 9/4 ($3.25) favourite.

Peter explains that there is a big difference between approaching a WFA race as opposed to a handicap event. With a big weight on his back, Peter had no plans to dictate to the field as was Vo's customary racing style. Peter says, 'You can plan for what you think is going to happen. Once those gates open the A plan may go out the door and you're looking for B and C plans. You just take it as it sorts itself out. I took it for granted that there was practically no way he was going to lead with nearly 10st [old scale] on his back from that alley and keep going, and keep going, and keep going until eventually we got to the front and I would have had no horse left. He would have been all used up.

'He settled midfield and I didn't have to bustle him, he was doing it easy because the speed was on, I just found ourselves in a nice position without having to force him to lead. He couldn't lead anyway. I nursed him, looked after him and kept him balanced, and took him up into the race. He ran them down and won well.'

That famous Cox Plate scratching of '88

With two strong wins under his belt and his fitness at peak level, Vo was all the rage for the WS Cox Plate of '88, a race in which he showed enormous courage 12 months earlier to finish fourth, after setting a sizzling pace that resulted in a new track record to Rubiton. Vic declared his wonder horse unbeatable for the event, but he also stated that his major worry for Vo was the track surface. That would seem a strange statement to make considering Melbourne was experiencing a very dry spring that year, and the previous three tracks Vo had raced on were rated Firm 2s. But as Team Vo would learn, track surfaces along with track ratings can be changed with the flick of a sprinkler system switch.

Three champion New Zealand horses Our Poetic Prince, Horlicks and Bonecrusher were all entered for the Cox Plate. There had been reports that the trainers of those horses had complained about the hard track surface. The officials at Moonee Valley ordered the track to be watered during the week leading into the Cox Plate. On top of the watering that had taken place in the early part of the week, the sprinklers stayed on for 40 minutes on the Wednesday. Then on the Friday night and early Saturday morning of the race, over 5ml of rain fell on the track.

Team Vo was quite annoyed about the amount of watering that was done to the Moonee Valley track and felt that the Moonee Valley officials showed favouritism toward the New Zealand horses. The official reason given for the heavy watering was that the weather bureau predicted high temperatures with strong winds on the Thursday, however those conditions never eventuated.

As a result, and despite a sunny day predicted, Vo was sensationally scratched from the Cox Plate on the morning of the race, a decision that brought with it enormous criticism from all corners and put Team Vo at odds with the Moonee Valley Racing Club. Vo was a huge drawcard, and his non-appearance was a disappointment for both the Club and Vo's loyal fans. Garry recalls Vo was 4/6 ($1.65) favourite.

Some 34 years later, the emotion in Garry Roberts' voice is still raw when I ask him to tell me about that day. 'There's only one story to tell. I walked the track four times. I walked it twice on the Friday before it rained, and then I walked it on race morning. I also walked it an hour before the Cox Plate with Shane Templeton.

'I was there at 7.30am with Jeff, Cyril and Vic at scratching deadline. We walked the track at 7 o'clock in the morning, we talked about it for 15 to 20 minutes and I said it's still too wet, he won't go as good, and Jeff agreed. That's why we scratched him.' Garry rated the track 'dead to slow (Soft)'.

Vic told Ron Taylor who wrote for the *Truth* newspaper that Vo would have raced at least six lengths below his best on that track surface, but if they were racing at Flemington that day, they would have run a record. Cyril agreed with Vic's assessment. It was his opinion that the track was worse than when Vo ran second last in the Manikato Stakes at Moonee Valley in August—the official track rating that day was a Soft 5. In relation to the Cox Plate track surface, Jeff says, 'We presented Vo for the race, the Club didn't present a track.' None of the Team thought the horse could finish in the top four placings on that track. With another Group 1 race a week away, they saw no point in putting Vo at risk. 'Moonee Valley did what they thought was right and we did what we thought was right,' says Jeff.

The Racing Australia database shows that races 1 and 2 that day were run on a track rated a Soft 5. After Race 2, the track rating was upgraded to a Good 3.

'Everybody was putting shit on me at the races because they said the track's dry, what did you scratch for?' Garry says. He walked the track one more time an hour prior to the Cox Plate and he still believed the true track rating was Dead to Slow (Soft). He had no trouble relaying his thoughts to the chief steward, Mr Pat Lalor. Garry says to me, 'You can take it down that until the day I die I'm still 100 per cent sure we did the right thing by scratching and the track was still Dead to Slow when the Cox Plate was run.'

A war of words erupted over Vo's scratching. After the race Moonee Valley CEO Ian McEwen, himself a New Zealander said, 'We didn't need Vo Rogue'. The three New Zealand horses ran one, two, three—Our Poetic Prince was first, Horlicks was second, and the mighty Bonecrusher was third.

Garry tells me that to this very day he is still defending the decision to scratch Vo from the Cox Plate. The bottom line is this: when comparing times across races run on WS Cox Plate Day in 1987

(Firm 2), 1988 (Good 3) and 1989 (Good 3), the times in 1988 were significantly slower across all distances. Additionally, Bonecrusher raced into 'equine immortality' in the time of 2-07.2 when he beat champion Our Waverley Star in the 1986 Cox Plate on a track rated a Soft 5. That is only 0.3 seconds slower than Our Poetic Prince's winning time. (table of Cox Plate Day race times, see p. 132)

Regardless of whether the stewards got it right in declaring a Good 3 track surface or Garry Roberts and the rest of Team Vo were correct in suggesting the track was Dead to Slow (Soft), the decision to scratch was made in the best interests of the horse. I will leave you with this. How many people do you know who own a racehorse with any ability at all, would put the horse first and foremost when there is $1.5 million on the table to share between the first four placegetters? I know two people: Jeff Perry and Garry Roberts!

The over-watering of the Moonee Valley track on Cox Plate Day was not quickly forgotten. Cyril and I attended a pre-Melbourne Cup function not long after; Garry was there too. There was a phantom call of the Melbourne Cup but in this version of the call, Vo was included in the race. The phantom race caller had Vo turning for home at Flemington 30 lengths in front of the rest of the field. He then declared, 'Oh no, the officials have run onto the track with their hoses and they are watering the track, ladies and gentlemen!' Everyone in attendance laughed and laughed, we all thought that was hilarious.

Upstaged by a female

The following week, Vo and Our Poetic Prince met at Flemington in the MacKinnon Stakes (WFA) over 2000 metres on a track rated a Firm 2. They went to the barriers as equal 6/4 ($2.50) favourites. When the field jumped from the barriers, Vo went straight to the front and at the 400-metre mark all was going to plan for Vo and Cyril. Sky Chase and Our Poetic Prince were chasing hard, but not hard enough. Back in the field, Empire Rose had two behind her in the field of 11 as her jockey pulled her to the outside to get a clear passage. She was still at least eight lengths off Vo. Once she got that clear passage her V8 engine kicked into overdrive and her strength came to the fore. She gathered the field in and swept past Vo in the final 20 or so metres of the race to win by half a length.

Vo ran second and Our Poetic Prince was two and a half lengths behind him in fourth place. Sky Chase split them in third place. The two favourites were upstaged by a female, the New Zealand mare Empire Rose, or 'Rosie' as her fans called her. She was a massive mare, standing at 17.1 hands and weighing 666kg. Rosie was a chestnut with a big white blaze and the daughter of champion New Zealand sire Sir Tristram. She was trained by master trainer Laurie Laxon and ridden by Tony Allen who was only 21 years old at the time. A runner-up to Kensei in the 1987 Melbourne Cup, Rosie hadn't won a race since the January of '88 and starting at the long odds of 66/1 ($67), she was not expected to worry either Vo or Our Poetic Prince. Rosie's win was reminiscent of Dandy Andy's Australian Cup boilover earlier in the year, but this time there was no 'goodness gracious me' or booing afterwards.

Cyril has always maintained that the only way horses could beat Vo on firm going was when they made a fast sweep past him close to the line. Horses that inched alongside him to challenge couldn't beat him because Vo knew they were there and he would just keep fighting to the line.

Three days later Cyril and I headed to Flemington as spectators at the Melbourne Cup. It was a great day. We were chaperoned from one marquee to the next and took a walk through the members car park where lots of obviously wealthy people sat at the boot of their luxury cars having a champagne and caviar picnic. I've never really understood that tradition—you know, going to the Melbourne Cup and sitting on a chair or picnic blanket in a car park. Everyone there seemed to be having a brilliant time though so there must be something in it.

Cyril and I got separated in the crowd as we went into the members stand to watch the Melbourne Cup. I had intended to back Rosie but ran into Maureen Olsen, Larry Olsen's wife. In brief chit-chat, Maureen told me that Larry thought Kensei was going into that year's race better than when he won it the year before, so I changed and backed Kensei instead. I ended up standing on an external stairwell in the members area somewhere opposite the winning post with a view across the track. It was a golden find and the best place to watch the race.

Kensei was well out of contention at the serious end of the race as Rosie skipped clear and looked to have the race well in her keeping. She had to call on every ounce of her strength to hold off the fast-finishing Natski ridden by Mick Dittman. I took enormous delight in cheering Rosie home and watching the celebrations from the stairwell. Her win over Vo in the MacKinnon had won me over. Rosie was awesome.

Vo went back to Brisbane to compete in the Listed Brisbane Handicap at Eagle Farm on 12 November. The race was sponsored by Qantas and Cyril wore their racing colours, red and white with the flying kangaroo.

It had been over a year since the locals had been given the opportunity to see their idol race on home turf and there was much excitement among his large fan base who had come out in droves to see him. Vo carried 61kg over the 1600 metre journey and started at 4/7 ($1.55). There was lots of talk about how far Vo would lead by, but Cyril had different ideas. Rather than take up the lead, Cyril settled Vo just off the pace in fourth position. Vo hit the lead soon after straightening and was immediately challenged by the smart galloper Don't Play who carried 9kg less. He was trained on the Gold Coast by Noel Doyle and ridden that day by Neil Williams. Cyril was confident Vo would hold Don't Play off and he did. Vo had close to a half-length to spare on the line and the local hero was cheered to a man as he sped past the winning post.

Winfield Stakes

Soon after winning the Brisbane Handicap, Vo was on a plane heading west to Perth. When Vo was scratched from the Cox Plate, the Western Australia Turf Club contacted Jeff and told him that Winfield, a tobacco company and major sponsor of sport in Australia, would like to sponsor Vo and the Team to go to Perth for Vo to race in the aptly named Winfield Stakes, a Group 1 (WFA) event run over 1800 metres at Ascot racecourse. The race was scheduled on 26 November.

The favouritism shown to Team Vo didn't sit well with some trainers in the east who whinged that Team Vo was getting paid to go over while others had to make their own way there with their horses and cover the costs themselves. One unnamed trainer labelled the sponsorship deal a disgrace and stated that the club should pay for everyone.

Well, that's just how it goes. If you have star appeal, people will pay for you to go to their event as the main attraction. If you don't and you still want to go and participate in the event, then you pay for yourself. If doesn't matter whether you are a sportsperson, movie star, singer, business leader or a horse, the more successful you are, the more star power you have, and the more bargaining power you have to name your price.

Sandra, baby Cymone, and I were guests of the Club and we spent the day on one of the tables somewhere in the members or committee area. It was truly an extravaganza. The food was exceptional, and every table had copious amounts of Winfield cigarettes on them for the guests. You won't see that today because sponsorship by tobacco companies was banned in Australia in the 1990s. I decided that I would smoke a cigarette to see what it was like. You won't see that today either. I didn't like it and I smoked it twice, first and last time.

While Sandra and I were being very well taken care of by the Club and sponsors, eating and drinking to our hearts delight, Cyril, Jeff and Vic were also being well looked after. The Perth racing fans flooded the racecourse, the press was clamouring to get photos and interviews, and Vo ... well, he just took everything in his stride. He travelled well to Perth, he settled in well, he was fit, and the track was rated a Firm 2. Carrying 58.5 kg, Vo started 4/9 ($1.45) favourite and with Cyril on board wearing the red and white Winfield racing colours, they won comfortably as expected. Following him across the line in second place was local three-year-old Our Bobby Boo, who under the WFA scale carried just 50.5kg. Eastern Classic, trained by David Hayes (son of Colin), was third.

Afterwards, Cyril and I went to the Burswood Casino Hotel where Garry Roberts threw a party in his beautiful suite and people just kept pouring into the place. It was meant to be for a few invited friends, but I think the bush telegraph came into play and it was soon packed with the press from every newspaper in the land, and other people who must have just followed them in. Garry was known as a successful punter and a high roller, and he was also a generous man.

Cyril didn't have a great deal to do with Garry, due mainly to the fact that Cyril mostly flew into Melbourne or Sydney on race day and flew home after the race, but we did have some lovely times in Garry's company. He hosted us at his family's magnificent Templestowe home one spring Sunday afternoon, and on another occasion after Vo had retired, when Garry was in Brisbane, he sent a limousine to pick us up and take us to Conrads Treasury Casino where he was staying. We had dinner, drank French champagne and returned by limo to the Gold Coast. On another occasion, Garry spent the day with our family and Jeff at our little farm and had a short ride on one of our horses. It was a great day.

The year 1988 finished well for Cyril. At the annual Queensland Jockeys' Association (QJA) Christmas Dinner, the QJA honoured Cyril with a lifetime membership award. He was treasurer of the Association back then and remains on the committee today.

CHAPTER 9

THE AUTUMN OF '89

The start of the Melbourne Autumn Racing Carnival saw a major gear change for Vo. The blinkers came off. The Team had formed the view that Vo had settled down in himself, but he was still over-racing. They thought that removing the blinkers would help him settle better in his races.

Vo's racing schedule was similar to the previous autumn, with two exceptions. Firstly, Vo would never again contest the Futurity Stakes, and that year, the Stanley Wootton Stakes over 1200 metres at Moonee Valley was added after the Australian Cup.

First up was the William Reid Stakes that Vo had won the year before. This year he was up against Zedative, a tough three-year-old chestnut colt trained in Melbourne by Angus Armanasco, who was long considered the best trainer of two-year-olds in the business. In his two-year-old year, Zedative raced 10 times and suffered just one defeat. That defeat came in the Golden Slipper on a wet track behind the Tommy Smith-trained Star Watch. Zedative started 13/8 ($2.60) favourite and ran unplaced. Zedative raced three times in the spring as an early three-year-old. He won the Ascot Vale Stakes and was then unplaced at his two subsequent starts.

Zedative commenced the autumn of '89 in great style winning the first running of the Group 2 Rubiton Stakes over 1000 metres at Sandown. Based on that run, Zedative—with regular rider Greg Hall in the saddle—was the even money favourite for the William Reid, while Vo's starting price drifted out to 6/1 ($7). Vo hadn't raced since his Perth win in November. We knew Vo could run a sub 1-10.0 for 1200 metres so if Zedative or any other horse in the race was going to beat him, they would have to better that. It was a good field of nine runners which also included Colin Hayes' flying mare Special who was in foal, and Redelva, himself a topline sprinter, so the likelihood of a sharp time on the Good 3 track was strong.

Vo jumped and led but he was under siege from Redelva who served it up to him in the middle stages of the race. On the home turn at Moonee Valley which has a very short straight of only 173 metres, Special ran to Vo. Redelva started to drop off and Special drew level with Vo and matched him stride for stride into the straight. The mare tried ever so hard but the strain started to tell, and she just could not get past him. In the final 100 metres of the race Zedative joined in three wide, and he and Vo drew away from Special. Zedative got the upper hand in the shadows of the post and got the 'bob' in on the line to win by a head. Special hung on for third in front of Redelva.

Not only did Zedative run under 1-10.0, he ran a new track record of 1-9.5.

It was a brave performance by the young colt, and he drew much praise from both his trainer and jockey. Greg Hall, who could be described as a polar opposite to Cyril, declared that there was no way Vo could beat Zedative. Cyril was more reserved and suggested that there was not a lot between the top horses racing at the time when they were all fit and well, and that Vo would hold his own with any of them.

Vo and Zedative didn't meet again. Zedative raced two more times that autumn and recorded wins in the Group 1 events the Lightning Stakes and the Futurity Stakes. He then retired to stud, having raced 17 times, amassing 14 wins—five of those at Group 1 level. Zedative went on to sire multiple Group 1 winners and also became a broodmare sire of note.

The following races leading into the Australian Cup were mere processions for Vo. The punting skill was more about determining what horse would finish second. The bookmakers had Vo at unbackable odds and Vic's catchcry, 'Good little horse isn't he, Vo Rogue', was heard week in week out as the adoring public filled the racecourses to cheer on their champion.

After Vo's second Orr Stakes win at 1/4 ($1.25) defeating Super Impose on a Firm 2 track, Vic stated that the decision to remove the blinkers had made Vo a better racehorse. Jeff and Cyril agreed.

'Vo would go hard from the jump, he only knew one speed and he would run his rivals ragged. As he got older and more experienced, he learned to pace himself better and relax in his races which allowed him to make another run to the line when challenged,' Cyril explains.

On the Monday after Vo's win in the Orr Stakes, Les Carlyon wrote, 'In the era of Fitzgerald inquiries, of bundles of funny money left on doorsteps like foundlings, the most honest act to come out of Queensland is a gelding with steel in his legs and iron in his soul.' (*The Age*, 13 February 1989.)

Mr Carlyon was a huge fan of Vo's. Jeff invited Mr Carlyon to meet Vo so he could gain an appreciation for himself as to the size and strength of the horse. Vo stood 16.3 hands and as Cyril puts it, 'He got bigger (not taller), and stronger as each season passed.'

One thing I learned from writing this book is that in that era of racing writers, Mr Carlyon stood head and shoulders above the other journalists. In reading and re-reading copious numbers of newspaper articles dedicated to Vo and that era of horse racing, I have formed a deep appreciation for Mr Carlyon's intelligence, insightfulness, humour, descriptive prowess, extraordinary ability to capture minute details that most others missed, and his superior skill as a wordsmith.

The next horse racing procession came one week following the Orr Stakes when Vo made it back-to-back wins in the Blamey

Stakes. Starting a 1/7 ($1.15) favourite on a Firm 2 track, the crowd started clapping and cheering Vo at the 400-metre mark of the long Flemington straight. He was well clear of Marwong who finished four lengths behind Vo, with Apollo Run another five lengths behind Marwong in third place.

By now, Vo's breeding, by a maiden out of a maiden, was making a mockery of the breeding scene in Australia, particularly in an age of the million-dollar yearlings. There wasn't much anyone could do about it though. On a flint-hard track and fully fit, as Mr Carlyon said, 'Vo was honest'. Added to that, Vo kept running time, he gave what he had, and he just kept winning. The St George Stakes was no different. He again started 1/7 and recorded back-to-back wins. At his prior two starts, Vo had seven others chasing him but in the St George he had only four.

The ridiculous ease of the win was well captured by race caller Greg Miles, whose description of the closing stages of the race left no one in doubt as to which horse owned the Autumn Racing Carnival in Melbourne during that period:

> Shakes up Vo Rogue with a hundred metres to go. It's a walk trot and canter for Vo Rogue. Here's win number 21. The Vo Rogue Show keeps rolling along.

Daylight ran second, but officially it was Super Impose some six and a half lengths away. Ideal Centreman was five lengths behind Super Impose and dear Dandy Andy was a further length behind him in fourth place. Celtic Air rain last.

* * *

Finally, the race everyone had been waiting for was upon us: the 1989 Australian Cup. There was no 'Vo Rogue can't win' coming from Jeff this time. The only danger looked to be the weather. Showers had altered the track rating from a Firm 2 to a Good 3 but fine weather was the order of the day for the Saturday race day on 11 March. Vo had retained his favouritism with bookies throughout betting, but he wasn't at the unbackable odds we had seen in his previous three races. He started at 8/13 ($1.60).

Some of the other trainers did not believe the contest would be in any way a one act affair. On the eve of the race, Our Poetic Prince's trainer John Wheeler was quoted by Keith Hillier in *The Sun* newspaper as having said, 'Our Poetic Prince has met Vo Rogue three times and beaten him twice. Vo Rogue is not unbeatable; in fact, I think he is overrated.' Wow, okay! The trainer also stated that he would instruct his jockey Noel Harris to bring Our Poetic Prince down the middle of the track because that's how Dandy Andy and Empire Rose beat Vo.

The same article quoted Super Impose's trainer Lee Freedman declaring the same, that is, that Vo was not unbeatable. I don't think too many—if any—Australian trainers thought Vo was overrated. There was renewed confidence in the Freedman camp for their horse because the week before, Super Impose raced and won over 2000 metres at Caulfield. In winning the Carlyon Cup, Super Impose broke the track record that had stood for 12 years.

There was also a new name in the form guide. European horse Highland Chieftain, trained by John Dunlop, was lining up for the first time in Australia. That horse was a prolific winner of Class races in Europe and he was coming off the back of a promising run in a Classic race in New Zealand. His jockey was Brent Thompson—yes that's right, the same Brent Thompson that won the race on Dandy Andy the year before. This year, Harry White was on board Dandy Andy who was trying to win back-to-back Australian Cups.

As the jockeys rode their mounts behind the barriers preparing to load, anyone looking for the famous brown jacket with white hooped sleeves and white cap would not have found them. Cyril was wearing different colours that day. Jeff had signed on with a sponsor, Souters. The company produced calf manna, a livestock supplement. Part of the deal was that Vo wore their colours in the Australian Cup and other races. The racing colours were yellow with green stripes in a pattern that looked like suspender belts, with brown striped sleeves and a yellow cap.

When the barriers opened, Super Impose took up the early lead but not for long. His jockey Darren Gauci took hold of him as Vo went around him and to the front. At the halfway mark, Vo and Cyril were five lengths in front of Dandy Andy, the party spoiler from the year before, with Super Impose and Our Poetic Prince racing together a length and a half behind him. Well into the straight and Vo had set such a fast pace that nothing from the back could make up any real ground. It was up to the three horses who had done the chasing from the get-go to raise another effort, but they were all out. Vo won the race by almost two lengths from Super Impose who came along the fence inside of Dandy Andy to nose out Our Poetic Prince, whose jockey rode to instructions and had him three deep to Dandy Andy's outside. Dear Dandy Andy ran a very gallant fourth two lengths behind Our Poetic Prince. Vo ran 2-01.6, just nine tenths of a second outside his metric track record.

We were all super excited and hoarse from screaming out to Vo and Cyril all the way down the straight. Cyril gave a few fist pumps as he brought his horse back to scale. While this time we had an abundance of confidence that Vo would win, we had learned from previous experience that nothing is real until it is. For Cyril, that win represented Vo's best effort. As Cyril often says, 'Choosing his best performance throughout his career kept on changing. Just when you thought he couldn't possibly step up any higher, he did.' Again, the very brilliant Les Carlyon best captured the scenes that followed. Below is an extract from *The Age* newspaper on Monday 13 March 1989:

Popular Vo makes a mockery of 'sport of kings' cliché

> … But, most important of all, the Rogue again made thousands of people happy. They rose from their seats and clapped with their hands above their heads. They waited around the mounting yard fence for the presentation, and

here was something. Racegoers usually regard this ritual as dull, not to mention dangerous because the speeches are sometimes so tedious that birds fall down dead from the sky.

Not this time. The Rogue himself is the most popular horse in Melbourne since Gunsynd. His connections enjoy a popularity that perhaps has no precedent. It is indeed more interesting to reflect on this cult rather than on the Australian Cup itself, which was little more than a fast procession.

Rogue is sport's best storyline: the street urchin who makes good. He is by Ivor Prince from Vow, who were both such fantastic gallopers they did not win a race between them, not even down the proverbial well.

The Vo Rogue Show, on the other hand, is by Runyon from Cinderella. That is why it has been a hit for three autumns and two springs. That is why, as John Cain, the Victorian Premier, said at the presentation, people were standing around 'savoring the occasion'. That is why Peter Armytage, the VRC chairman, was able to talk of 'what surely must be known as Vo Rogue day'.

Vo smashed the $2 million prizemoney barrier. Ingolby wines of McLaren Vale created a premium port blend to honour his achievement. Not too many horses can boast their own port label.

Vo backed up the next week in the Stanley Wootton Stakes at Moonee Valley over 1200 metres. The run was a pipe opener to maintain his fitness for the Sydney campaign. Vo started 7/4 favourite. Coming off a paralysing win over 2000 metres just seven days earlier, Vo was no match at that stage of his preparation against out and out sprinters, but he gave the race everything he had. Vo ran fourth behind Jet Fighter, beaten just three lengths. Groucho and Grandiose finished second and third. The rain came to Sydney and Vo's campaign there was aborted. Vo came home to spell in the Queensland autumn sun in the care of Bobby Gill.

Vo Rogue on horse float leaving Nudgee Beach August 1987.
Vo was being followed and photographed everywhere he went. Vic was never one to be worried about keeping up appearances.
Photo: Noel Pascoe

Top: Vic and Rode Rouge at the Brisbane Ekka August 1984.
Middle: Vo and Jeff at Hendra November 1984 a few weeks after Vo arrived at Vic's stables. Jeff described Vo as looking like a big Great Dane dog.
Bottom: Debby, Vo and Vic at Doomben racecourse – late 1986.
Photos: Debby Osborne

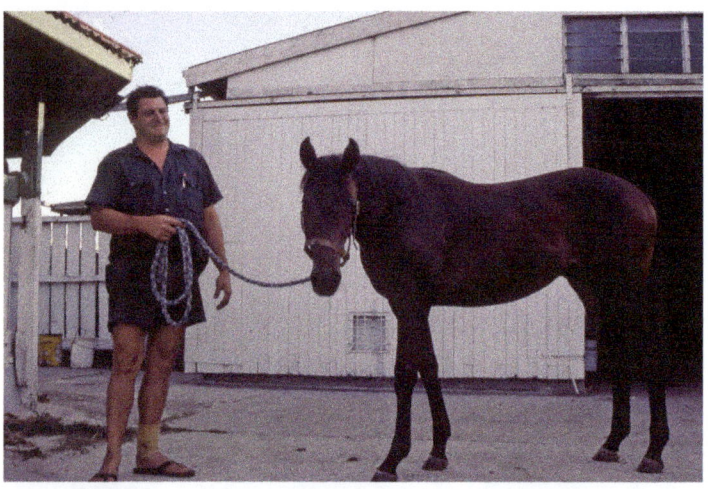

Top: Vo is all alone at the winning post as he wins his first race in Melbourne, the Creswick Stakes at Flemington on 9 March 1987. *Photo: Colin L Bull*
Bottom: Vo and Cyril on the steeple course at Flemington after the Creswick Stakes on 9 March 1987.
No, Vo wasn't contemplating a career over the jumps, but our son Braidon thinks Vo would have been a ripping ride over the live hedges at Casterton. Vo's half-brother by Semipalatiinsk called Vowtinsk ran second in the 1999 Grand Annual at Warrnambool and two months later he won the Grand National at Flemington in race record time.
Photo: Lynlea Small

Top: Cyril with our spectacular painting by Rick Sinclair (oil on canvas—1800 x 1200mm). Vo and Cyril's first Group 1 win, the 1988 William Reid Stakes at Moonee Valley on Australia Day, 26 January 1988. *Photo: Lynlea Small*
Bottom: Vo and Vic after Vo's record-breaking win in the 1988 St George Stakes. Caulfield 27 February 1988. *Photo: Bruno Cannatelli @ ultimateracingphotos.com.au*

Futurity Stakes Day 1988 – Caulfield 5 March 1988

Top: Vo and Campaign King go hammer and tong to the line with Vo winning the Group 1 Futurity Stakes in track record time.
Photo: Bruno Cannatelli @ultimateracingphotos.com.au
Bottom: Vo, with his head lowered, is led around the parade yard after his win in the 1988 Futurity Stakes. Elite journalist Les Carlyon gave a critical observation that, 'The gelding blew badly on return to scale, was soaked in sweat from shoulder to rump, and tucked up for about 10 minutes or so.' *Photo: Colin L Bull*

Australian Cup Day 1988 – Flemington 14 March

Top: Vic, me, Jeff and Cyril walk onto Flemington racecourse for the 1988 Australian Cup.
Bottom: Vo stares out into a sea of people who have gathered to get a close-up view of their turf idol.
Photos: Colin L Bull

Australian Cup Day 1988 – Flemington 14 March

Bonecrusher's fans made it very clear how they thought the race would pan out.
Photo: Colin L Bull

Australian Cup Day 1988 – Flemington 14 March

Vo and Cyril head onto the track for the 1988 Australian Cup. A sea of smiling faces line the fence to wish their hero good luck.
Photo: Colin L Bull

Australian Cup Day 1988 – Flemington 14 March

Flemington grandstand and lawn are absolutely jam packed for the Match Race of the Century, the 1988 Australian Cup.
Photo: Colin L Bull

Australian Cup Day 1988 – Flemington 14 March

Top: To the racing public, the unthinkable has happened. 125/1 rank outsider Dandy Andy races past Vo in the closing stages of the race to cause one of the greatest boilovers in Australian racing history.
Middle: The smiles have disappeared except for that on the face of 'The Babe', Brent Thompson who is delighted as he brings Dandy Andy back to scale.
Bottom: Trainer Jim Cerchi, then aged 76 and father of 13, pulled out a piece of note paper and quickly scribbled, *'Come on Dandy Andy'* as his giant killer returns to scale.
Photos: Colin L Bull

Giant mare Empire Rose storms past Vo near the line to win the Group 1 MacKinnon Stakes at Flemington on 29 October 1988. The margin was half a length. Three days later, she won the Melbourne Cup.
Photo: Colin L Bull

Qantas Brisbane Handicap Day – Eagle Farm 12 November 1988

Top: Crowd waiting for Vo to arrive on course at Eagle Farm for the Qantas Brisbane Handicap. It had been more than a year since he had raced in Brisbane and his loyal fans were keen to get a look at their local hero.
Bottom: Garry, Vic, Jeff and Cyril talk tactics prior to the Qantas Brisbane Handicap.
Photos: Noel Pascoe

Sir Edward Williams, then Chairman of the Queensland Turf Club presides over the presentation to Team Vo after the horse won the Qantas Brisbane Handicap beating smart Gold Coast trained galloper Don't Play.
Photo: Noel Pascoe

Australian Cup 1989 – Flemington 11 March

Top: Vo alone on the line in the 1989 Australian Cup. He had 1.5 lengths to spare from Super Impose with Our Poetic Prince third.
Photo: Colin L Bull
Bottom: Vo made amends for his defeat in the 1988 Australian Cup when he came out the following year and defeated Super Impose, Our Poetic Prince and Dandy Andy to win the 1989 version. Garry, Cyril and Jeff were delighted with their star galloper's performance. *Photo: Martin King/Sportpix*

Top: With 600 metres to go in a 1010-metre flying handicap at Doomben, Vo was eight lengths off the lead with one horse behind him. He wasn't going to let his fans down. He put his V8 engine into overdrive, rounded them up and won running away beating handy sprinter Newington Butts. 5 August 1989. *Photo: Noel Pascoe*

Bottom: With the cavalry coming and Randwick racecourse rocking, Vo holds off Groucho and Don't Play in the Group 1 George Main Stakes to post his one and only win in Sydney. 23rd September 1989. *Photo: Steve Hart Photographics*

St George Stakes Protest – Caulfield 24 February 1990

Top: Vo beats King's High by three quarters of a length. Soon after, jockey Michael Clarke lodged a protest.
Middle: Champion trainer Colin Hayes and his stable jockey champion Michael Clarke await the outcome of the protest hearing.
Bottom: Vic's face says it all. Protest upheld. Vic had plenty to say about that but all to no avail.
Photos: Colin L Bull

CHAPTER 10

THE SPRING OF '89

Vo's spring campaign of 1989 started off at Doomben on 5 August in a 1010 metres Flying. He had four opponents including the flying machine Newington Butts. Vo carried the top weight of 59kg while the other horses carried the minimum 50kg. Again, Vo wore the racing colours of the sponsor, Souters. Vic made a gear change, the crossover nose band came off for the first time in Vo's career. Its purpose is to stop horses from pulling. Vo wasn't going to be pulling in this race.

At the 600-metre mark Vo was about eight lengths off the leader with only one horse behind him. Coming into the home turn, Vo started to quickly round up the opposition and won, running away by a length and a quarter with Newington Butts second. Cyril puts that win up there among his best for the pure reason that 1010 metres was not Vo's go, but in the end class prevailed.

Of that win Cyril recalls, 'I was pretty worried before the home turn that we might not get there. We were at least eight lengths off the lead, but once we straightened, I knew he'd win. He made up a lot of ground from the 400 metres to the 200 metres. I was confident then he would pick them up.'

Four days later, Cyril was back at Doomben to ride Gazon Roi, trained by his brother Warren and part-owned by his father Bob. The result was vastly different to that of the Saturday before. I was watching the race from our house which overlooked Doomben at the 1200-metre mark and had a view from the top of the straight to well past the winning post.

At the 200-metre mark, Gazon Roi suffered a heart attack and died. The horse crashed through the inside running rail into the infield. Cyril was thrown clear of the horse, but it looked like a very heavy fall. I was horrified. Despite being heavily pregnant with our first child, I immediately drove over to the races.

By the time I got there Cyril had walked back to the casualty room and the press had gathered around him. Vo was entered for a Flying handicap only three days later on the Saturday, and with Cyril looking a little worse for wear, the press was keen to know the full extent of his injuries, and probably more importantly to them, if he would be fit to ride Vo.

Just prior to the fall happening, I was speaking with Jeff who was at our place looking after Vo. The handicapper had given Vo 59kg and the rest of the field had 49kg. That included Lord Penn who was a prolific winner in open company over sprinting distances. Jeff was not impressed at having to give Lord Penn a 10kg weight advantage and he told me he would not accept with his horse.

With the press asking Cyril a range of questions about how he felt, and would he ride Vo on Saturday, I leaned over to Cyril and whispered to him, 'Vo's not starting.' I could see he was relieved to hear that. It wasn't up to me to tell the press. Jeff and Vic held court in matters that were Vo and press-related. The press found out with everyone else: at acceptance time. Cyril came out of the fall relatively unharmed, bar for a few scratches and bruises. He was very lucky that day.

Having missed the flying, Vic entered Vo for the Warwick Stakes (WFA) at Warwick Farm in Sydney on 19 August. There was a bit of a problem for Cyril though. The jockeys in New South Wales were locked in dispute with the Australian Jockey Club over liability insurance cover and the jockeys had gone on strike. Until the matter was resolved, no senior jockeys would ride at any meetings in New South Wales. Cyril told Vic and Jeff that while the jockeys were on strike, he wouldn't ride Vo in New South Wales. He had already refused rides at the Murwillumbah meeting the day prior.

The NSW Jockeys' Association agreed that they would grant Cyril an exemption to ride Vo because Vo was trained outside of New South Wales and therefore not a part of the dispute. They did place a restriction on his exemption though, and that was that Cyril was not to accept rides from other trainers.

Cyril would not take advantage of his interstate colleagues' kind offer, and instead stood beside them in solidarity for their cause. For Cyril, it was a matter of principle. Cyril told Max Presnell from *The Sydney Morning Herald* newspaper, 'I'll stick with the jockeys. It has always been the case as far as we [Queensland jockeys] are concerned that if there is a strike on anywhere we won't ride there … you've got to do what you think is right and I won't be riding him if there's a strike on.'

From my observations and experience over many years, the jockeys' associations across Australia are the strongest associations in racing. Despite the cut-throat approach to gaining rides and the competitiveness of race riding, when it comes to matters of an industrial nature, most jockeys live by the motto 'all for one and one for all'. Sure, there are a few renegades who break ranks and do their own thing, you get that in all walks of life and industry. But largely, jockeys stand side by side in solidarity for one another. Most jockeys would have made great musketeers alongside Athos, Porthos, Aramis and d'Artagnan.

It would be remiss of me if I didn't also add that the jockeys are supported and advised by some of the best minds in the country who work with the Australian Jockeys' Association (AJA) and State bodies.

The jockeys are also very fortunate to be supported by the National Jockeys' Trust (NJT) when they face tough times. Once a jockey, always a jockey and the NJT does a marvellous job providing a range of support for past and present jockeys and their families.

Back to the Warwick Stakes and as it turned out, Vo didn't run in that race. The rain came down and Vo remained in Brisbane for another two weeks before heading south.

On 25 August Cyril and I were overjoyed to welcome our beautiful son, Daniel James into the world. Daniel is a wise old soul, I'm sure he's been here before. He has a very special gift with horses, bonding quickly with them and gaining their trust almost instantly.

I was very unwell for a long time after Daniel's birth. It was not an easy birth, and I was in hospital for 10 days. Within a week of being discharged I was rushed back to hospital by ambulance with severe mastitis, an infection in the milk duct of the breast. By the time Daniel was four months old, I weighed 46kg. Cyril was back and forth to Sydney and then Melbourne nearly every weekend and when he was away, I often had a friend or family member spend the day with Daniel and me.

* * *

Vo had his first start that spring in Sydney on 2 September in the Tramway Stakes (Group 3) followed by a run in the Theo Marks Stakes (Group 2) one week later. Vo finished unplaced in both runs on Firm 2 tracks, but he was only four lengths or so from the winner each time. Finally, on 23 September 1989, Vo shook his 'maiden' tag in Sydney and won his first and what would be his only race there. But what a race to win. Vo won the time-honoured Group 1 George Main Stakes (WFA) over 1600 metres at Randwick, beating Groucho by a neck with Don't Play a long neck away third. It was a crack field as it is every year in that race, and it was a tremendous win. Vo had to call on all reserves to get there.

My favourite race caller of all time John Tapp OAM called the race which can be relived on YouTube. In the final 50 metres of the race, with the cavalry coming on both sides of Vo, it looked like Vo might not hold them off. But John gave the perfect description of the finish of the race when he said, 'Vo Rogue in front he's got a heart as big as himself, he'll win, Vo Rogue. Vo Rogue has cracked it at last in Sydney.' The Sydney punters on course cheered Vo from the home turn to the winning post and they gave the 10/9 ($2.10) favourite a hero's welcome back to the winner's circle.

The headline read 'Farewell Rogue …'

Immediately after that win, Vo went to Melbourne to prepare for the WS Cox Plate. Just one week after his George Main Stakes glory, Vo made a third attempt to win the John F Feehan Stakes. He was considered unbeatable in a field of four runners and as expected, he started the short price favourite at 4/9. However, a win was not to be. New Zealand horse Our Westminster—trained by Ngaire Fraser and ridden by Harry White—spoiled the party. Coming to the home turn, Our Westminster drew alongside Vo and they bumped. The New Zealander then moved ahead of Vo and halfway down the straight he hung in and cut Vo off. Cyril stood up in the stirrup irons and was forced to stop riding Vo and take hold. In doing so, Vo bumped the running rail and lost ground. Our Westminster ran past the winning post two and three-quarter lengths ahead of Vo with King's High one and three-quarter lengths behind Vo in third place.

Cyril fired in a protest and although the interference to Vo was obvious, the margin was too great to warrant reversing the result. The stewards found Harry guilty of careless riding and suspended him for 13 days. He was not particularly happy about that, and Harry told Cyril that he deserved an Academy Award for his acting performance on Vo.

A week later when lining up to win his third successive Turnbull Stakes, Vo ran fourth in a field of five behind Super Impose. Vo started the 5/4 favourite. That defeat was followed by a third in a field of 14 behind Almaarad in the Caulfield Stakes (Group 1). Vo started at 6/1 on a Good 3 track. He was beaten just over two lengths. It was a top-class field that included Vitalic who ran second, and The Phantom, Dr Grace and Super Impose who all followed behind Vo. A return to form seemed on the cards and just in time because the next race was the WS Cox Plate, the race Vo had been targeted for all along.

Cyril and I were, and still are, friends with Michael Kerr who was stable jockey for Greg Mance. As well as being a topline trainer, Greg was also the owner of the Windsor Smith shoes empire and had a stable complex with an apartment across the road from Flemington racecourse. Greg also had a racing complex on the Gold Coast where he was based. I was still recovering from childbirth and multiple breast infections, and Cyril had a very heavy schedule riding Vo in Melbourne that spring. Michael invited the three of us to stay with him in the apartment for a few weeks which was great. The day before the WS Cox Plate, Daniel—at the age of nine weeks old—and I flew to Melbourne with Cyril.

Michael and Greg had a lot of success together, and at that time, Michael was riding Cole Diesel who was getting ready for the Melbourne Cup and had won the Group 1 Toorak Handicap and Group 1 Caulfield Cup double. Unbelievably, Moonee Valley chief executive Ian McEwen denied Cole Diesel a place in the field for the Cox Plate that year reasoning that the horse was not a weight for age horse, he was a handicapper. Cole Diesel was relegated to first emergency. As expected, Vo made it into the Cox Plate field.

Melbourne's predictably unpredictable weather arrived on the Thursday morning prior to the Cox Plate with very heavy rain falling. That was followed by gale force winds. Tom Brassell writing for the *Daily Mirror* on Friday 27 October suggested that the weather would most likely decide the result, but on a good track, he thought that Vo would win and if so, 'it will be one of the most popular victories an Australian racecourse has ever witnessed.'

On Cox Plate day the track rating was a Good 3. Almaarad was the clear favourite at 11/4 ($3.75) with Vo starting at 5/1. The Team was once again confident about Vo's chances and took the view that if they didn't think he could win it they wouldn't be there.

The WS Cox Plate race always attracts the best WFA stayers in the country and that year was no different. The result, however, was something that we didn't expect and hadn't even contemplated. Vo barely participated in the race, he was never in it. He never looked likely at any time. He beat just one horse home and that horse was Zabeel. Almaarad won the race but had to pull out everything he had to overpower Stylish Century in the shadows of the post. Empire Rose came from well back to nose out Our Westminster for third.

Jeff offered no excuses, but Cyril had Vo's back. Cyril said that the track was a bit greasy in the early part of the race and Vo slipped and slid at the 1200-metre mark and after that he wouldn't put in. Jeff countered that it didn't really matter that he slipped and slid because Vo wasn't doing anything in the race prior to that anyway. Vic agreed with Cyril's assessment of Vo's run, noting that Vo had done that previously when he wasn't happy with the track surface. Naturally, everyone was disappointed. Of course we were. But as Cyril liked to remind anyone who would listen, Vo was not a machine and too much was expected of him too often.

In reference to Vo's poor performance, the headline in the *Sunday Herald* Sport section on 29 October 1989 read like an obituary. Below is an extract from that article written by Trevor Grant:

Farewell Rogue, you were one of the greats

But once they jumped it became as clear as the Waterford jug on the winner's dais, that it is just not the same any more.

By the 800m with the challengers leaving him behind, Small was wielding the whip at a furious rate in a desperate hope that the old spark might suddenly fire. Nothing, though, could stop the march of time.

It was all over for the Rogue. The trouble is that even for racecourse realists like Perry, it is hard to face. 'I'd just like to see him going out on top, not at the back end of the field,' Perry said.

Wouldn't we all?

Over the years I've given a lot of thought to Vo's dislike for tracks that held any water at all, and this is what I have come up with. Have you ever walked along a smooth cement footpath in the rain wearing a pair of thongs that no longer has any grip left on the sole? I have. I slip and slide everywhere and have no confidence in my footing. I take little steps to ensure I don't fall over. I always feel like I'm going to dislocate one or both knees. That's how I have always imagined Vo felt when he raced on a track that had any wetness to it. He had no confidence to stride out and was protecting himself from injury.

* * *

Despite the shock and disappointment of Vo's performance in the Cox Plate, his campaign continued. Vo's next run was in the MacKinnon Stakes on the Saturday before the Melbourne Cup. Vo raced better at Flemington than he did at any other track, and it was hoped that he would return to something like his old self, particularly as the track was rated a Firm 2. It was also Victoria Derby Day and for me, probably the best day of Flemington's four-day Spring Carnival event. Putting that race day ahead of the Melbourne Cup race day says a lot. Derby Day is my second favourite race day of the year behind Cox Plate Day.

Our young baby Daniel and I went across to Flemington for an hour or so to watch the Derby and the MacKinnon which were run back-to-back. It is a much different experience having a baby in a pram at a big event to being on your own. We couldn't get within cooee of anything and while every vantage point was taken to watch the Derby, Daniel and I found a seat under a tree 30 or 40 metres from the fence that formed the outside running rail in the straight.

With Stylish Century being a Queenslander, I was cheering for him in the Derby. It was very hard to hear what was going on but as the horses thundered past the area where Daniel and I were sitting, I caught a glimpse of Stylish Century's colours many lengths clear of the rest of the field. He won the race by four lengths. It was a terrific win, particularly after the hard run he had only one week earlier in the Cox Plate.

Next up was Vo's race. It was a high-quality field headed by two of New Zealand's champion mares, Empire Rose who started the 4/1 favourite, and Horlicks who started at 9/2 ($5.50). It was a hit and run mission for Horlicks. She had no other races scheduled in Australia and it was her lead up race to the 2400 metres Group 1 Japan Cup. King's High, Super Impose and Australia's Champion Horse of the Year from the previous season, Research, were also lining up in the field of 13. The bookies had Vo at 13/2 ($7.50), and while they kept him safe, it was still the longest price he had been since the Feehan Stakes in the September of '88.

Vo took charge of the race and lead the field early, ever increasing his lead as the race continued. Well into the straight and King's High started closing in on Vo and at the 150-metre mark, he had collared Vo but then Horlicks stormed past the two of them and she went on to score a soft win, beating King's High by half a length with Vo a further length behind him in third place. Super Impose was fourth, a length behind Vo, and Rosie was a long neck away in fifth place. Horlicks ran a super time for the 2000 metres event in recording 2-00.3, making Vo's performance a very good one. Vo had bounced back. He didn't win the race, but he did prove that his career wasn't dead after all.

To make Vo's performance more meritorious, Horlicks went on to win the Japan Cup in a race record time of 2-22.2 and in doing so, she became the first Australasian horse to win the Japan Cup. Horlicks was trained by father and son team Dave and Paul O'Sullivan and ridden by Dave's son (Paul's brother), Lance O'Sullivan.

Three days later was Melbourne Cup Day. Cyril had two early rides at Flemington that day, both of them for Vic. He finished down the track on Pictain in a 1000 metres two-year-old race and down the track again in a straight six race on Making Mischief. It didn't matter that the horses ran unplaced—it was just a great experience for Cyril to ride at the Melbourne Cup meeting and it was a great experience for the horses. It was a much more subdued event that year compared to the one before. Daniel and I went to the races to watch Cyril's two events and then we went back to Greg's apartment to cheer Michael and Cole Diesel on.

The disappointment Greg and Michael felt in missing out on a Cox Plate run was followed up with what appeared to be a poor performance from Cole Diesel in the Melbourne Cup. As one of the favourites for the great race, the grey didn't fire a shot at any time. Michael explained to me that unfortunately, while in the barriers, Cole Diesel lashed out and hit the barrier with his hind leg causing a similar effect to smacking your funny bone.

When the barriers opened the horse couldn't get himself coordinated and was tailed off for most of the race. He passed some tired horses in the straight, but the circumstances were a great disappointment to both Greg and Michael. Prior to the race they shared a strong confidence that they could win. The Melbourne Cup that year was won by Tawrrific; Super Impose ran second and The Phantom ran third.

The jockey copped a right royal bagging

Vo's final race in the spring of '89 was in the Queen Elizabeth Stakes (Group 2), a handicap event over 2500 metres at Flemington. Vo was having his first start over that distance—the furthest he had ever raced was 2040 metres. He had to race over an additional 460 metres more than he had ever previously gone and he had to carry 59.5kg as well. Being a handicap event, and at that stage of his career, Vo had to carry a great deal more weight than the rest of the field. After Vo's weight, the runner with the next heaviest weight was Power of Destiny who carried 52kg. The rest of the field carried between 49kg and 51.5kg.

Vo started the 13/4 ($4.25) favourite and tried his very best. He found himself in a head-to-head battle with It's Candide at the busy end of the race. She was carrying 51.5kg. Just as Vo got the better of her, Our Shannon Lad (also carrying 51.5kg) came with a sweeping run over the top of them and won, running away by three quarters of a length to Vo. It's Candide battled on bravely to finish a short half head away in third place.

The headline in the *Sunday Sun* the next day read, 'Owners at odds over Small ride'. Max Presnell reported that, 'Part-owner Geoff Roberts [a typo], was critical of jockey Cyril Small's tactics.' He quoted Garry as having said, 'If he was ridden properly he might have won.' The article went on to say that Garry thought that Cyril should have used Vo's speed more and also quoted him as having said, 'After all, he [Vo Rogue] was only running against a field of hacks today.'

The roasting also made headlines in Brisbane's *Sunday Mail*. Bart Sinclair reported:

Rogue jockey given whipping by owner

Minor part-owner Gary Roberts yesterday publicly 'bagged' Brisbane jockey Cyril Small over his handling of Vo Rogue who finished a gallant second in the Queen Elizabeth Stakes at Flemington.

In the wake of Vo Rogue's narrow defeat by New Zealander Our Shannon Lad, rumours swept Flemington there has been a major blow-up in the Vo Rogue camp. Roberts in a television interview after the event, admitted Vo Rogue had not been ridden in the way he felt it should have been to give it the best chance of winning.

'I wanted the horse ridden quietly early but then to speed up from the 1200 metres and get a big break,' Roberts said. 'Cyril Small did not do this and it allowed the other horses to get to him and he was beaten.'

Garry never spoke to Cyril about his ride on Vo in the Queen Elizabeth Stakes, but Cyril spoke to Jeff about the comments published in the newspapers. Jeff told Cyril not to worry about what was in the papers; he was very happy with the ride and in his opinion, weight beat the horse, not the ride. The weight difference of 8kg over the 2500 metres proved, in Jeff's opinion, to be the number one factor in Vo's defeat.

I think it's also important to reflect on Cyril's comment about Vo not being a machine. Vo had his first race start for that campaign in the first week of August and raced in the Sydney and Melbourne Spring Carnivals in the best races against the best horses in the land. While his form was mixed, he did win a Group 1 in Sydney and was placed in two Group 1 events and two Group 2 events in Melbourne. By the time the second week of November came around, Vo was entitled to be a little fatigued and he was soon on the drive back to Bobby Gill's property for a spell.

* * *

While Vic was busy preparing Vo for another Autumn Carnival, Cyril had a flying start to the New Year—literally. On New Year's Day, he gave punters what should have been the ultimate tip about his opinion of first starter Abcadan in a two-year-old race at Eagle Farm. Like Ancaro, Abcadan was trained by Merv Lewis. Cyril hired a helicopter to take him from the Gold Coast races to Eagle Farm but was held up along the way and went within a breath of being replaced on Abcadan by Jamie Bayliss, who was an apprentice at the time.

Cyril was runner-up in in the fourth race at the Gold Coast on Appleton Lad and fired in an unsuccessful protest, putting Cyril behind time to make the Eagle Farm race. The stewards officiating at the Gold Coast called forward to Ray Murrihy at Eagle Farm to give him the heads up that Cyril was running behind schedule but was on his way. Cyril was pleased to see Merv come out to meet him and open the gates to the course proper from the infield where the helicopter landed. Abcadan duly scored an impressive win at the juicy odds of 7/1 ($8), leaving the odds-on favourite from Sydney, Tipperary Wizard in his wake.

Cyril often hired helicopters to take him from one racecourse to another when there were two race meetings held on the same day and he had what he considered strong winning chances. I remember him flying from Murwillumbah to Ipswich, from the Gold Coast to the Sunshine Coast on multiple occasions, and from Brisbane to Toowoomba. For a while there it became a semi-regular thing if Cyril thought the horses were good enough. Cyril started using the same helicopter service and pilot and enjoyed more than anything else taking the opportunity to take the controls and fly the helicopter himself for a few minutes on each ride.

CHAPTER 11

THE AUTUMN OF '90

By the time the 1990 Autumn Carnival in Melbourne was ready to kick off, it is fair to say that Vo Rogue was so popular in Victoria, had he run for Premier of the State, he would have recorded a landslide victory. That statement is in no way intended to be disrespectful to former Premier John Cain or his successor. The Victorian racing public adored Vo and despite his winless Melbourne spring, he was still their champion. That's not to say he wasn't loved by the public in other states—he was. Just that in Victoria, they had adopted him as their own, along with his connections.

Having said that, some people from different corners of racing had come out of the woodwork and were happy to state their opinions that Vo's best days were behind him, and that was their prerogative. Trevor Grant, as mentioned earlier, led the way after Vo's miserable run in the WS Cox Plate the previous spring. But here's the thing: champions, whether they be horses or people, have a special knack for putting sceptics in their place, and one thing we all know about Vo, he was a champion.

The Autumn Carnival of that year would prove to be perhaps the most controversial of Vo's racing career. Between the sprinklers coming on again to overwater Flemington and a protest verdict described in the media as 'beneath contempt', circumstances surrounding Vo that autumn gave the press plenty to write about, and in doing so, the battle lines were drawn. Team Vo, the racing public, and many from the press it seemed were on one side, while it appeared that the stewards and to some extent the racing administrators were on the other.

Vo kicked off proceedings on 29 January in the William Reid and dead-heated with Redelva for fourth. They finished just under one and a half lengths from the winner, New South Wales sprinting sensation Lightning Bend, trained by Gerald Flick at Coffs Harbour on the Northern Rivers. Wayne Harris rode the winner who ran the super time of 1-09.0 and in doing so, recorded a new track record and his first and only Group 1 win. Only 14 months earlier, Lightning Bend recorded his first win at his second race start at Bowraville racecourse, a tiny country track also on the Northern Rivers. He had come a long way in a short period of time. Well done to him and his trainer.

Twelve days later, Vo became only the second horse, behind Manikato, to win three CF Orr Stakes. He beat his old rival Super Impose by one and a half lengths with King's High a further two lengths away in third place. The race was run on a track rated a Good 3. Vo's connections breathed a sigh of relief that their horse was once again in the winner's stall. Jeff even joked that he couldn't remember where the winner's stall was.

Vo's legion of loyal fans backed him into 7/4 favourite and gave him a standing ovation as he returned to the saddling enclosure. Those who had written Vo off must have been having second thoughts and we were all very happy that Trevor Grant had gone the early crow some three months earlier with his 'Farewell Rogue …' headline.

After the Orr Stakes win, Vic stated what we all knew about Vo and that was, 'he's just better in the autumn'. Cyril had an equally measured view about his good mate and said, 'He's only a horse, they have their bad days like anyone else.'

There were more bad days ahead for Vo, but they were not due to poor performance. Vo was looking to emulate his three CF Orr Stakes wins in the Blamey Stakes and the St George Stakes that were his next two race starts, but other elements would come into play that would feature strongly against him.

Just one week after Vo returned to the winner's stall in spectacular fashion, he was at his favourite track, Flemington, trying to make it a hat-trick of wins in the Blamey Stakes. He was 4/7 in a field of six runners on a track rated a Firm 2. His two main rivals were up and coming star Better Loosen Up (also known as BLU) trained by Colin Hayes, and Super Impose. Vo was a shoo-in to win, well at least that's what everyone thought.

Due to the extreme heat in the days leading into the race, the sprinklers came out and the track was heavily watered, then the showers of rain came on race morning. Sound familiar?

The stewards were confident they had rated the track correctly, but had they? Cyril didn't think so. The flying clods of dirt in previous races were some giveaway, but Vo's defeat into third place behind BLU and Super Impose in a time of 1-37.6 was further proof that the Firm 2 rating may have been an error. Vo's previous wins in the Blamey, both on tracks rated a Firm 2, recorded a 1-34.0 record in 1988 followed by a 1-35.9 time in 1989. BLU's time was 1.7 seconds slower than Vo's slower time.

When Vic walked into the mounting yard after the race, he pointed to the semaphore board that had the winners, margins and times on it and said, 'Look at the time. That tells the story. The sprinklers were on all the time and there was too much watering.'

Cyril asked Super Impose's jockey Darren Gauci how he would rate the track and Darren replied, 'I would say it's Dead.' Cyril was sure the damp track had beaten Vo. The official records on the Racing Australia database show that the Blamey Stakes, race 3 on the card, was run on a Firm 2. Immediately after, the track was downgraded to a Good 3. Race 5 on the card was the Australian Guineas run over 1600 metres and won by champion three-year-old Zabeel in a time of 1-37.3. I'll let you be the judge as to what you think the true track rating was.

The horse racing rivalry between New South Wales and Victoria is as old as the country itself. In the era that Vo raced, the ethos of freedom of the press was alive and well. Clive Galea who called himself the 'Stay-at-home punter' wrote for the Sydney-based *Sunday Telegraph*. Despite Vo being a Queenslander, Mr Galea had no issues taking a clear shot at the Victorian Racing establishment about their overwatering of Flemington, as reported in the 25 February 1990 edition of the *Sunday Telegraph*. Mr Galea wrote:

The ghost of bigots past

Anyone who saw the movie Phar Lap would have been surprised at the savage serve it gave the legendary Victoria Racing administrator L.K.S. MacKinnon. I originally thought the filmmakers had indulged in a little poetic licence as they portrayed him as an autocratic so and so who obviously believed God was a Victorian squatter and a VRC member.

Ordinary folk (like Phar Lap's connections) were expected to run their horses at his carnival but were not expected to have the gall to win. With Sydney-based jockeys absolutely blitzing the Melbourne hoops and interstate horses dominating, it was a very happy coincidence that Flemington was overwatered last week, thereby greatly diminishing the chances of both Vo Rogue and Show County (despite the fiction of 'track fast' rating).

Of course, the Vo had similar bad luck before a recent Cox Plate when connections scratched the horse after the Valley had also been overwatered in error.

If this sort of miscalculation continues, this modus operandi could well become known as 'the Melbourne fair go'. Shelley Hancox and other dedicated Victorians would no doubt claim you cannot beat bad luck. Other punters a touch more cynical and from north of the border would lean more to the theory that the ghost of L.K.S. MacKinnon is alive and living in Toorak.

Despite the obvious disappointment, there was only one thing Team Vo could do and that was to put the race behind them and move on to the next one, the St George Stakes. That race was run just one week after the Blamey and Vo only had three opponents: Marwong and King's High that had met Vo many times before, and Bronze Knight, a very handy galloper, but not in the same class as the others.

Vo went to the post a 1/2 ($1.50) favourite on a track rated a Good 3. Vo led into the home turn and for a few strides, upon straightening he rolled off the fence. Michael Clarke riding King's High went for the run that presented itself, but Vo rolled back in before he could take it. Marwong raced up and got to within a neck of Vo with King's High directly behind Vo. Cyril got to work and rode hard. Vo responded and kicked away from Marwong.

Michael appeared content to sit behind Vo and Marwong waiting for a run to appear between them. He had every opportunity to pull his horse across heels to the outside of Marwong, but chose otherwise. The run finally came for King's High and he passed Marwong to his inside. Cyril was not overly vigorous on Vo in the final stages of the race and as they neared the winning post, he was just waving the whip at Vo and they beat King's High by three quarters of a length. The margin would have been greater had Cyril pushed Vo harder to the line. Marwong was a further length behind in third place with Bronze Knight fourth, eight lengths behind Vo.

As the horses came back to scale, Michael Clarke fired in a protest against Vo. Bookmakers betting on the protest outcome had Vo at long odds-on to keep the race. Colin Hayes, trainer of King's

High, was confident that his horse would gain the race on protest. He was correct.

Vic was very vocal and said his horse had been 'robbed' and asked the question, 'If Michael Clarke was going well enough to beat Vo Rogue on the home turn, why didn't he pull back and around Marwong then?' Mr Hayes countered, 'They took his running and that's all there was to it.' (Clem Dimsey, *The Sunday Telegraph*, 25 February 1990.)

Jeff had no problem voicing his disappointment about the protest verdict and said, 'As you slide down the banister of life, that's just another splinter in the arse.' Jeff and Vic then threatened to boycott the upcoming Australian Cup with Vic saying, 'We might as well go to Sydney rather than lose races this way down here.'

So controversial was the ruling that Chairman of Stewards Pat Lalor made the unusual decision to explain to the nation via Sky Channel, just why he and his panel upheld the protest. Mr Lalor stated that he and his panel were of the opinion that there was ample room for King's High to take the run on the inside but Cyril, riding with the whip [in the right hand], allowed Vo to roll back in and chop King's High off. With King's High disappointed for a run, that horse lost ground and was then blocked for a run all the way down the straight until approaching the winning post.

Mr Lalor and his fellow stewards believed that King's High got within a length of Vo and when Vo shifted in, Vo took the run that rightfully belonged to King's High. That incident, together with the fact that he was held up due to losing that run, cost King's High the race. The incident accompanied by Mr Lalor's comments is on YouTube if you want to see it for yourself.

Cyril has always maintained that King's High would never have beaten Vo had he either got up on the fence or his jockey taken him to the outside of Marwong. Cyril reasoned that King's High wasn't coming with a sweeping run like Dandy Andy, Empire Rose and Our Shannon Lad did when they beat Vo. Cyril believes that at best, King's High would have run to Vo and challenged him, but Vo would have kept fighting to the line and held King's High at bay. After all, that's how Vo beat Fair Sir in the Turnbull, Campaign King in the Futurity, and Groucho in the George Main Stakes.

Despite their threats to abandon Melbourne and head north to Sydney, Jeff and Vic decided to remain in Melbourne with Vo to contest the Australian Cup. 'We were there and ready for the race. The goal was always the Australian Cup,' recalls Jeff. As was expected, the field was as hot as they come and it was considered one of the best WFA events run in Melbourne for many years. Notable opponents to Vo included BLU, Super Impose, The Phantom, Kingston Rule (a son of the American superstar Secretariat) and King's High. But the favourite for the race at 2/1 ($3) was star three-year-old colt Stylish Century.

Like Vo, Stylish Century commenced his career in Queensland. Like Vo, he was a bold front runner. Like Vo, he could also run time—very fast time. For example, he ran 1-08.34 for 1200 metres in the Golden Nugget Stakes in the February of '89. He smashed the track record that day. In Almaarad's Cox Plate in the spring, Stylish Century led everywhere but the post to be beaten just a head into second place. The closest Vo got to Stylish Century in that Cox Plate was three lengths off him at the 700-metre mark before Vo started to go backwards. Stylish Century beat Vo home that day by more than 13 lengths.

The colt then came out and gave nothing else a chance in the Victoria Derby before beating two home in the Melbourne Cup, then briefly headed to the spelling paddock. When he resumed from his spell in the William Reid, Stylish Century ran third and beat Vo home by half a length. Stylish Century finished fourth behind Zabeel in the Australian Guineas before thrashing Zabeel by six lengths in an all the way win in the Autumn Classic over 1800 metres.

Stylish Century's owner Dick Monaghan didn't mind moving his colt from one trainer to the next. Noel Doyle and Bart Cummings both had a turn at training the horse, but Bill Mitchell prepared him for the Australian Cup. Mr Monaghan had reportedly formulated a plan for his horse to win the race in record time. While Team Vo had a healthy respect for the young colt who had a 5.5kg weight advantage over Vo, Vic rightly pointed out that the colt had two things against him going into the race: he hadn't won in open company, and he hadn't won at WFA.

On the Sunday afternoon before Monday's race, Jeff and Vic walked the track. It was rated a Good 3 but they wanted to find out for themselves. In certain areas between the barriers at the 2000-metre mark and the 1400 metres, the track was cut up on the inside section and slightly wet in patches. Vo drew barrier nine in a field of 10.

As the newest recruits to the School of Hard Knocks, Team Vo had completed their homework in readiness for their final exam. They had a few scores to settle and this time they were hatching their own plan. This time, they would leave nothing to chance. This time, there would be no opportunity for stewards' intervention, or claims of track tampering. This time, only the tough would prevail. For Team Vo, it would be all or nothing.

The Team stood together in the mounting yard as the jockeys were about to be called to mount up. Jeff's instructions to Cyril were simple and clear. 'When you jump, fire Vo up and let him go. Stay out wide and make a straight line to the 1400-metre mark where the track starts to turn. Then bring him across to the fence.' As Cyril started walking away to mount Vo, Jeff added, 'Oh, and Cyril, break their hearts.'

Stylish Century drew barrier two and we thought for sure his jockey Kevin Moses would attempt to take him to the lead from the jump. Stylish Century outpaced the other runners, but Cyril was out wide on the track riding to instructions and riding hard on Vo. At the 1800 metres, Vo was one and a half lengths clear of Stylish Century.

Vo and Cyril stayed out deep on the track and at the 1400 metres where the track starts to turn, Cyril brought Vo onto the fence. He was five lengths clear of Stylish Century with Kingston Rule eight lengths behind him in third place. Vo had the field strung out over 20 or more lengths—or close to 80 metres.

Halfway down the straight, Stylish Century was brave but no match for the older horses. Vo was still four lengths in front with BLU and Super Impose emerging from the pack, but all to no avail.

As Vo steamed past the winning post the crowd went wild and roared in appreciation of his demoralising win. This was the day that the people's champion reminded everyone why he was the people's champion, and Vo gave some of the best racehorses in the land a masterclass in horseracing. He showcased the qualities that made him the most exciting and most loved racehorse in the country at that time, and in doing so recorded his greatest victory.

Vo had a length to spare to BLU, followed by Super Impose, Stylish Century and The Phantom; five lengths behind The Phantom in sixth place was King's High, eight lengths behind Vo. Kingston Rule ran seventh. Bruce Clark writing for *The Courier Mail Sport* summed it up best when he wrote, 'He hammered his knockers into silence and rivals into submission.'

Vo had given his fans and everyone connected with him some of the most thrilling moments in their lives on a racetrack, but that Australian Cup win, that was the pinnacle. A winless Melbourne spring, talk of the great horse being past his best, record attempts thwarted by an overwatered track and a questionable protest outcome. By the time the 1990 Australian Cup came around, despite Vo being out of favour in betting, Vo's connections felt the pressure more than any other time in the horse's career, but they believed in their horse, and they believed in each other.

As Cyril brought the horse back to a Melbourne Cup-like reception, Vic was excitedly telling anyone that would listen about his betting escapades. 'I backed the horse at 8/1 ($9), I went back into the ring after I saddled him and backed him again at 12s ($13). You wouldn't believe it, I went back again just before the race and got 14s ($15).'

Jeff was brimming with pride and in reference to the recent

disappointments, he said, 'I guess you could say the splinter came out today.' When asked to comment on Vo's performance, Jeff said simply, 'The horse has said it all. If he never wins another race, he has answered his knockers.' Indeed he had.

Brendan Cormick later reported in *The Australian* that in running the time of 2-00.9, Vo had registered 60.04 seconds for the first 1000 metres and 60.05 for the last 1000 metres. Extraordinary!

Jeff and Vic hadn't called their horse a champion, but surely this would change their minds. 'Would you call him a champion now Jeff?' Cyril asked him as he walked Vo into the winner's stall.

'Don't say too much yet Cyril, we've still got the swab,' Jeff cheekily replied, not able to resist having a dig at the stewards and alluding to the fact that the stewards still had another chance to change the result. Jeff would later say that he couldn't call his horse a champion because he couldn't handle wet tracks, but Jeff did say that Vo was a very very good horse.

Once Vic calmed down from the excitement of his betting prowess, he summed up how we all felt when he said, 'I've never had a greater thrill with him than today because he went into this as the underdog.' Vic went on to say it was his most satisfying win in the 32 years he had been working with racehorses. Jeff, Cyril and Garry echoed that sentiment.

Before the race, Garry had conceded that he thought Stylish Century would probably lead and win. He rated Vo a 6/1 chance and at the lucrative odds of 12/1, he backed Vo. In giving his post-race assessment, Kevin Moses told the press, 'He [Vo] went along so fast I just thought he had to stop. I was going faster that I wanted to just to keep in touch. He broke my heart chasing him.' (Bruce Clark, *The Courier Mail*, 13 March 1990.) Jeff tells me that Kevin said to him, 'They told me I was on a champion, if that's the case I don't know what you would call the horse I was chasing.'

When asked if Stylish Century would run in the Alister Clark Stakes five days later at Moonee Valley, Bill Mitchell told Keith Hillier from *The Sun* newspaper, 'It's a little difficult to make a decision when you're so stunned.'

For the record, Stylish Century did go to the Alister Clark and started a 4/5 ($1.80) favourite. He gave everything he had and tried valiantly to hold off Zabeel who went into battle with him from the point of the turn to the winning post. Zabeel prevailed by a nose. Zabeel would go on to become one of the most influential and successful stallions in modern times. Stylish Century in contrast had moderate success at stud.

The Australian Cup celebrations went on for days and superlatives were being thrown at Vo left, right and centre. The press has a great memory, and some have an even better sense of humour, including cartoonist Ron Tandberg who perhaps had the last word on Vo's tumultuous Melbourne autumn.

This cartoon by Mr Tandberg appeared in The Age newspaper on 13 March, the day after Vo's magnificent win in the 1990 Australian Cup. King's High finished in sixth place, eight lengths behind Vo. Tandberg poked fun at the stewards and generally summed up the public opinion of the St George Stakes protest result.

Cyril's daring ride on Vo in the Australian Cup did not go unnoticed. He received a Caltex Sports Star of the Year Qualifying Award for the month of March. It was an 11 out of 10 ride after all. Across that year, there was a record 46 monthly nominations covering

20 sports. Sponsored by *The Courier Mail* newspaper, the finalists and winner were announced at a function held at The Sheraton Hotel in Brisbane in the November of that year. Cyril was invited and he duly attended. It was an honour for Cyril to have been nominated as the calibre of sports stars for that year was truly outstanding.

The Courier Mail reported that golfer Wayne Grady was named Caltex Sports Star of the Year and the other 11 finalists were Peter Senior, golf; Glen Housman, swimming; Lisa Curry, swimming; Hayley Lewis, swimming; Rob Parrella, lawn bowls; Greg Norman, golf; Trevor Hendy, surf lifesaving; Chris Munce, turf; Simon Doyle, athletics; Mick Doohan, Grand Prix motorcycle racing; and Mal Meninga, rugby league.

After the Australian Cup, The Vo Rogue Show moved north to Sydney as planned. Despite Vo's customary 'catch me if you can' tactics, he was no match for the opposition on a wet track (Soft 5) at Rosehill in the Group 1 Segenhoe Stakes and finished midfield, some eight and a half lengths behind BLU.

Vo was stabled at Kembla Grange for his Sydney campaign and was being prepared for the George Ryder Stakes, also at Rosehill one week later. After the Segenhoe, Jeff went back to Brisbane. It had been pouring rain and Jeff told Vic if the training tracks were too wet, he was to take the horse to the beach to do his fast work. With the rain still coming down, the course manager at Kembla Grange offered to allow Vic to gallop Vo on the actual racecourse but told him he would have to stay out wide on the track if he did that. Vic accepted the offer.

As Vo was pulling up and rounding the turn out of the home straight, the horse faltered and lengthened the tendon that runs into the near side fetlock. And that was the end of that campaign. Jeff went back to Kembla Grange and brought Vo and Vic home.

CHAPTER 12

THE BEGINNING OF THE END

I remember vets coming and going from the stable. The news wasn't good. The general consensus was that the injury was likely career ending. Jeff and Vic treated Vo and with a long spell, plenty of beach work and swimming, Vic got him back to the racetrack.

Vo campaigned briefly in Brisbane and Melbourne in the late spring before heading to Perth for a hit and run mission in the Winfield Stakes. He was one run short and finished fifth—two lengths behind Bar Landy, trained by Peter Ilsley in the Victorian town of Seymour.

Then it was back to Brisbane to compete in the feature races of the Summer Carnival. Vo performed well without winning, finishing third on two occasions from three starts, all in Listed races. He was never far from the winner, but he wasn't the same horse. The Vo Rogue of old would have eaten every one of those horses he competed against for breakfast.

While Vo was out of the winner's circle, Cyril was not. He won the $100,000 Listed BATC Stakes for two-year-olds at Doomben on 100/1 ($101) shot Unbid Slam for trainer Peter Blackwell.

While Vo battled to overcome his injury and regain his best form, BLU was busy building his champion status on a global scale. He won the Feehan Stakes, Turnbull Stakes, Cox Plate and MacKinnon Stakes in the Melbourne spring of 1990 before conquering the world in the Japan Cup.

From Brisbane, Team Vo headed south in that January of '91 for what had become a ritual campaign. The William Reid, then the CF Orr Stakes, the Blamey, the St George, and the Australian Cup. Cyril and Vic had a spring in their step having tasted success on the Tuesday before the William Reid with Bell's Best winning a 1000 metre handicap event at Sandown.

However, their good fortune would turn to misfortune when six days later Vo suffered interference from another runner early in the William Reid and was put out of contention. That interference aggravated Vo's old injury.

Jeff explains that after the William Reid, when Vo was galloped to maintain his fitness levels, he would be sore in the near side fetlock and favour that leg. He would be fine within three days of the gallop, but because Vo was such a good doer, he needed a regular sprint up to keep his fitness levels high. To overcome the problem of missing work while his fetlock settled down, Vic thought he would be able to keep the horse sound by swimming him. 'Vicky gave it his best shot, but it didn't work,' says Jeff.

There's no doubt that the initial injury caused Vo to lose several lengths in ability, at least six according to Jeff, but his heart would not lie down. Vo continued to show the courage and fighting spirit that we all applauded and loved him for, but as Jeff says, 'When you are in that grade you can't have anything go wrong.'

Vo saw out the autumn in Melbourne running third in the Orr Stakes and running the bravest of races when second to BLU in the Blamey Stakes. BLU who came from behind in his races, ran Vo down in the final 30 metres of the race to win by a long neck after Vo set up his usual commanding lead. Vo beat two home in the St George

Stakes as the 4/6 favourite before he gave everything he had, but he was no match for the newly-crowned Australian champion BLU in the 1991 Australian Cup. BLU beat Vo who ran second by five and a half lengths, and in doing so, BLU recorded his seventh straight victory, four at Group 1 and three at Group 2 level.

Vo raced three times in the Brisbane Winter Carnival, all without success. The 1990 Australian Cup, his greatest win ever, proved to also be his last. Strangely enough, the 1991 Australian Cup would be the final win in BLU's stunning career. He bowed his tendon while preparing for the Sydney Autumn Carnival of that year and despite a long spell and his team doing the best they could for him, he never reached the dizzy heights of his 1990/91 season. BLU retired in February 1993 to Living Legends in Melbourne and passed away in March 2016.

The sun set on Vo Rogue's racing career at the same race track it started, the Gold Coast Turf Club. The date was the 20th May 1991. The race was the Listed Southport Cup over 1800 metres run on a track rated a Soft 5. He ran sixth in a field of seven, and was beaten just under seven and a half lengths. Vo was seven years old.

The winner of the race was New Zealand horse Rough Habit, or Roughie as he would later become known to his legion of fans. In a sense, Vo passed the baton to Roughie that day as Roughie, trained by John Wheeler, would go on to create a cult following of his own on both sides of the Tasman. In particular, the Queensland racing public adopted him, and he made the Queensland Winter Racing Carnivals his own from 1990 to 1993. He didn't attend the Carnival in 1994 but in 1995, when it looked like his best days were behind him, he came out in a field of 20, jumped from barrier 19 over the 2400 metres at Eagle Farm and absolutely trounced the opposition to win the Group 2 O'Shea Stakes at WFA with local champion jockey Shane Scriven in the saddle. The racecourse erupted. It was awesome.

Just like Vo, Rough Habit's parents never won a race between them. Looking back, there were so many similarities between Vo and

Roughie. In his book, *Rough Habit: an unlikely champion*, author Ken Linnett wrote:

> Rough Habit came from humble beginnings, bred as little more than a hobby, via a free service, to an unfashionable imported sire, Rough Cast, from the unraced mare Certain Habit. The resultant colt's stature suggested that the experiment was doomed to fail. His breeder, Isabell Roddick, said of Rough Habit, the foal: 'He was … probably not the best looking, but I didn't think he was as hideous as he's been made out to be. He was a very small horse. But looks don't tell you if they're going to win a race.'

For Vo's ever-faithful senior part-owner Jeff Perry, Vo's retirement was a relief. Jeff said many times that the fun of having the horse is not always there when you have a champion. 'While it's lovely to have a champion, it gets to the stage where people expect too much from him and the media call at all hours of the day and night, your life is no longer your own,' says Jeff.

Vo never won Australian Champion Racehorse of the Year, an award voted on by racing administrators and the media, although in 1989 he was a close runner-up to Research. Vic always maintained that had the public voted, Vo would have won the award at least three times. I have to agree with that. Vo did win Queensland Horse of the Year on three occasions: '87, '88 and '89.

Contrary to Tony Meany's prediction that Vo would never beat a champion horse, well I repeat what I said earlier: champions have a special knack of putting sceptics in their place.

Campaign King was already considered a champion sprinter-miler when Vo beat him in the Futurity. Our Poetic Prince was crowned New Zealand Horse of the Year in the 1988/89 season, the same season he ran third to Vo in the 1989 Australian Cup.

Super Impose was inducted into the Australian Racing Hall of Fame in 2007; however, for the most part of his racing career when up against Vo, Super could only chase him. Super came into his own after Vo sustained that injury at Kembla Grange. Super gave some of the most spectacular performances on a racetrack one could ever wish to see. He won two Doncaster Handicaps, two Epsom Handicaps, two Chipping Norton Stakes, a Ranvet Stakes and a WS Cox Plate—all Group 1 events. I really loved that horse.

Better Loosen Up was crowned Australian Champion Racehorse in 1991 and inducted into the Australian Racing Hall of Fame in 2004. Yet Vo gave him, and Super Impose, a galloping lesson in the 1990 Australian Cup. BLU, I loved him too—who didn't?

And let's not forget 'Big Red', the mighty Bonecrusher who ran third behind Vo's second to Dandy Andy in that eventful Bicentenary Australian Cup, deemed the 'Match Race of the Century'. Bonecrusher won 10 Group 1 races, and in the 1986/87 season was awarded both the New Zealand and Australian Horse of the Year titles. In 2010, he was inducted into the New Zealand Racing Hall of Fame. Bonecrusher was a champion, no doubt about that.

For me, Vo raced in an era of champions. It was a privilege to watch so many great horses race one another, and to see them evolve into the individual champions they became, finding their own places among the greatest racehorses in Australian and New Zealand Racing history.

In remembering Vo, Robert Craddock writing for *The Courier Mail* on 21 August 2010 gave this description of him:

> Vo Rogue was the champion who redefined horsepower. Calling him a racehorse never quite did him justice. A freight train with a saddle on top … that's more like it.

I asked specialist equine vet Dr Lester Walters who owns and operates the Eagle Farm Equine Hospital why, in his opinion, Vo was such an outstanding racehorse. Dr Walters treated Vo as a weanling soon after he arrived at Vic's, when he had a minor injury to one of his back legs. Even then, Dr Walters was impressed by the young horse and he followed Vo's career with great interest.

Dr Walters explains that Vo was an incredible athlete with a big stride and there were four key factors that contributed to his greatness. Firstly, Vo had extremely strong physical structures—that is, tendons, bone, muscle, lungs and heart. Secondly, the rhythm of his galloping action was perfect. Thirdly, he had exceptional athletic balance. Even when leading in Group 1 events, Vo did it so easily, he was so well balanced and never out of rhythm. Above all else, he was mentally tough.

Cyril has been asked many times about Vo's racing style and what made him so superior. His response is always the same. 'Vo won his races by running his opposition off their legs. They would make a run at him at the 200 metres or, if at Flemington, at the clock tower, but the other horses were tired from chasing him and they couldn't go on. At that point, Vo was still going as good as ever and more often than not, he would hold them off.'

Legendary Italian trainer and breeder Federico Tesio is famous for having said, 'A horse gallops with his lungs, perseveres with his heart, and wins with his character.'

Who would have thought that the weedy weanling best described as Erk, whose parents didn't win a race between them, would grow to be the horse that would not only personify Tesio's statement, but with it, capture the hearts of the Australian racing public and become the people's champion?

CHAPTER 13

STATISTICS OF INTEREST

Many high-profile industry stakeholders consider that Vo was far more effective racing anticlockwise (Melbourne and Perth) than he was racing clockwise (Sydney and Brisbane). Cyril supports that view and explains that the horse was sometimes inclined to move away from the inside rail to the left when racing clockwise. When racing anticlockwise, the rail was there to keep him straight. Also, sometimes when Vo raced in Sydney, he was coming off the back of a rigorous Melbourne campaign where he had raced week in week out and broken race and track records; he was often at the end of his campaign. And, on occasion, the tracks were softer in Sydney than what he raced on in Melbourne. The conditions and circumstances were mostly not as favourable when Vo raced in Sydney as they were when he raced in Melbourne.

When Jeff called time on Vo's career, he had raced 83 times and amassed 26 wins, 14 seconds and nine thirds with prizemoney totalling $3,116,100. Vo won six Group 1 races, and 10 Group 2 events plus a Listed win. The Turnbull Stakes and CF Orr Stakes have since been upgraded from Group 2 events to Group 1s. Under today's rankings, Vo's Group 1 record would stand at 11. Additionally, Vo raced across and won black type races in four states: Queensland, New South Wales, Victoria and Western Australia. He won 14 races on Firm 2 tracks and 12 races on Good 3 tracks. Of his 26 race wins, nine of them were racing in the clockwise direction. Vo was the first Queensland-trained racehorse to win $1 million in prizemoney. He was a superhorse, but wet tracks were his kryptonite.

I am a bit of a stats buff, so I have placed some interesting stats below for you to consider. I want to highlight the tracks on which Vo won his races.

Vo Rogue – Number of starts on racecourses in order of the greatest number of wins

Racecourse	No. of Starts	First	Second	Third	Unplaced
Flemington	18	7	6	3	2
Caufield	10	4	2	2	2
Doomben	11	3	1	2	5
Sandown	6	3	–	1	2
Moonee Valley	12	2	3	1	6
Gold Coast	9	2	1	–	6
Eagle Farm	3	2	–	–	1
Ascot	2	1	–	–	1
Randwick	2	1	–	–	1
Ipswich	1	1	–	–	–
Sunshine Coast	2	–	1	–	1
Rosehill	5	–	–	–	5
Canterbury	1	–	–	–	1
Murwillumbah	1	–	–	–	1
Total	83	26	14	9	34

Source: Racing Australia database

Vo won the greatest number of races at Flemington, however, he also raced on that track more often than he raced on any other track. He raced at Flemington on 18 occasions and while he won seven races there, he also achieved six seconds and three thirds. Vo was unplaced only twice at Flemington—those losses came in the Craiglee Stakes in the spring of '88 and the Turnbull Stakes during his winless Melbourne spring of '89.

While Flemington was then regarded by many as the premier track in Australia, and arguably still is today, and is home to the Melbourne Cup, the stats show that Vo was very versatile regarding his ability to win on tracks of all shapes and sizes. Vo was the track record holder over 2040 metres for one season at Moonee Valley, and won a William Reid at that track over 1200 metres, however, the stats show that Vo also suffered the most unplaced runs of his career at Moonee Valley alongside the Gold Coast, where, to be fair, Vo did his early racing and during that time was just learning the game.

Vo raced nine times in New South Wales on four different tracks and was successful only once. That was at Randwick. The other eight times he was unplaced.

How bizarre to look at the table on the previous page and see that Vo had one run on a country track (Murwillumbah, NSW) and was unplaced. You may recall me telling you earlier that the day he raced at Murwillumbah the track was a Heavy 10. Astonishingly, three months later, Vo ran back-to-back track records at Flemington and Moonee Valley. Has there ever been a champion galloper who simply could not pick his feet up in the wet to the extent that Vo Rogue could not?

The table on p.131 shows that while we often think of Vo as a topline stayer, he was an equally effective sprinter and miler. Vo won five races, including Group 1s, over each of the distances of 1200 metres, 1400 metres and 1600 metres.

Vo Rogue – Wins by distance and Group level

Distance	Wins	G1	G2	Listed
1010m	1	–	–	–
1200m	5	1	–	–
1350m	1	–	–	–
1400m	5	1	3	–
1600m	5	1	2	1
1800m	3	1	2	–
2000m	5	2	2	–
2040m	1	–	1	–

Source: Racing Australia database

More on the Cox Plate Scratching of '88

As already discussed, Vo was sensationally scratched on the morning of the 1988 WS Cox Plate due to the state of the track. Connections believed the track was wetter and softer underfoot and that the Good 3 track rating was incorrect. They gave the horse no chance of winning on the track that was presented. Our Poetic Prince won the race in a time well outside what would be expected to be run on a track rated a Good 3.

Vo's part-owner, professional punter and racing analyst, Garry Roberts, continues to defend the decision to scratch Vo from the Cox Plate to this very day. Curiosity got the better of me so I thought I would take a closer look at the times that were run on Cox Plate Day 1988 and compare them with times run on Cox Plate Day the year before and the year after.

Firstly, it is important to understand that Cox Plate Day brings together the best racehorses in Australasia, and in more recent years, some of the best racehorses in the world. For that reason, it can be argued that there shouldn't be a major discrepancy between times when the track ratings are the same.

To enable a clearer picture to appear, I have created a table below that compares not just race times for the three Cox Plates of 1987–89, it compares race times across a range of distances for races run on those days. All races selected for this analysis are Group races. In 1987 the track rating was a Firm 2 and in 1988 and 1989 the track ratings for those events were a Good 3.

Cox Plate Day race times 1987, 1988 and 1989.

Year	Race	Status (Group)	Distance	Track Rating	Time	Winner
1987	A.J. Moir Stakes	2	1000m	Firm 2	0-56.7	Placid Ark
1988	A.J. Moir Stakes	2	1000m	Good 3	0-58.6	Scarlet Bisque
1989	A.J. Moir Stakes	2	1000m	Good 3	0-56.9	Clay Hero
1987	The Crystal Mile	3	1600m	Firm 2	1-34.4	Tierra Rist
1988	The Crystal Mile	3	1600m	Good 3	1-36.9	True Dreams
1989	The Crystal Mile	3	1600m	Good 3	1-34.6	Fendalton
1987	W.S. Cox Plate	1	2040m	Firm 2	2-02.9R*	Rubiton
1988	W.S. Cox Plate**	1	2040m	Good 3	2-06.9	Our Poetic Prince
1989	W.S. Cox Plate	1	2040m	Good 3	2-03.2	Almaarad
1987	Moonee Valley Cup	2	2600m	Firm 2	2-42.9	King Matthias
1988	Moonee Valley Cup	2	2600m	Good 3	2-46.4	Ideal Centreman
1989	Moonee Valley Cup	2	2600m	Good 3	2-42.2	Sydeston

* Track Record
**1988 Vo Rogue scratched due to the state of the track

What we find is that in 1987 in all events except for the Moonee Valley Cup, the times were faster than those run in 1989 by between 0.2 and 0.3 seconds. Those results are expected because the track surface was firmer in 1987.

Now, if we compare the times for the races run on a Good 3 track in 1988 and a Good 3 track in 1989, we find the following differences:

1000 metres, 1.7 seconds slower in 1988; 1600 metres, 2.3 seconds slower in 1988; 2040 metres, 3.7 seconds slower in 1988; and 2600 metres, 4.2 seconds slower in 1988. If we take the slower time of King Matthias in the Moonee Valley Cup in 1987 and compare that time with the time run for that race in 1988, there is still a difference of 3.5 seconds.

Also, remember that Bonecrusher raced into 'equine immortality' in the time of 2-07.2 when he beat champion Our Waverley Star in the 1986 Cox Plate on a track rated a Soft 5. That is only 0.3 seconds slower than Our Poetic Prince's winning time.

So, there you have it. What do you think now? Was the track on Cox Plate Day 1988 a Good 3? Did the stewards get it right or were Garry Roberts and the rest of Team Vo correct in suggesting the track was Dead to Slow (Soft)? Can we even compare race times on the same track from one year to the next?

I will leave it with you to make up your own mind. No doubt this will make for a good debate over a social drink on a Sunday afternoon, and hopefully give Garry Roberts a break from having to defend the decision some 34 years later.

Vo Rogue's Racing Career by Wins Only

Date	Age	Racecourse	State	Race Name	Race Type
25 Jun 86	2	Eagle Farm	QLD	–	2YO Maiden
27 Dec 86	3	Gold Coast	QLD	–	Set Weights
3 Jan 87	3	Gold Coast	QLD	–	Set Weights
21 Jan 87	3	Doomben	QLD	–	Progressive
9 Mar 87	3	Flemington	VIC	Creswick Stakes	3YO Open
14 Mar 87	3	Moonee Valley	VIC	Alister Clark Stakes	3YO Group 2
29 Aug 87	4	Doomben	QLD	TAB Silver Anniversary	Open Handicap
5 Sep 87	4	Ipswich	QLD	Ipswich Fourex Flying	Flying
3 Oct 87	4	Flemington	VIC	Turnbull Stakes	Group 2 SWP
26 Jan 88	4	Moonee Valley	VIC	William Reid Stakes	Group 1 WFA
6 Feb 88	4	Sandown	VIC	CF Orr Stakes	Group 2 WFA
13 Feb 88	4	Flemington	VIC	Blamey Stakes	Group 2 WFA
27 Feb 88	4	Caulfield	VIC	St. George Stakes	Group 2 WFA
5 Mar 88	4	Caulfield	VIC	Futurity Stakes	Group 1 WFA
1 Oct 88	5	Flemington	VIC	Turnbull Stakes	Group 2 SWP
15 Oct 88	5	Caulfield	VIC	Richard Ellis Plate	Handicap
12 Nov 88	5	Eagle Farm	QLD	Brisbane Handicap	Listed
26 Nov 88	5	Ascot	WA	Winfield Stakes	Group 1 WFA
11 Feb 89	5	Sandown	VIC	CF Orr Stakes	Group 2 WFA
18 Feb 89	5	Flemington	VIC	Blamey Stakes	Group 2 WFA
25 Feb 89	5	Caulfield	VIC	St. George Stakes	Group 2 WFA
11 Mar 89	5	Flemington	VIC	Australian Cup	Group 1 WFA
5 Aug 89	6	Doomben	QLD	BMW Australia Quality	Flying
23 Sep 89	6	Randwick	NSW	George Main Stakes	Group 1 WFA
10 Feb 90	6	Sandown	VIC	CF Orr Stakes	Group 2 WFA
12 Mar 90	6	Flemington	VIC	Australian Cup	Group 1 WFA

SP- Starting Price   MR - Metric Record   SWP - Set Weights & Penalties

Jockey	Weight (kg)	Distance	Track Rating	Time	SP	Prizemoney
Cyril Small	51	1200m	Firm 2	1-11.10	5/1	2000
Larry Allen	51	1200m	Good 3	1-11.22	9/2	3000
Larry Allen	52.5	1600m	Good 3	1-37.49	2/1	3000
Larry Allen	54.5	1350m	Firm 2	1-20.30	11/8	2000
Cyril Small	55	2000m	Firm 2	2-00.70MR	4/1	19,500
Cyril Small	54	2040m	Good 3	2-03.40R	4/1	130,000
Cyril Small	55.5	1200m	Firm 2	1-09.70	5/1	11,700
Cyril Small	55.5	1200m	Good 3	1-10.10	7/4	10,500
Cyril Small	55.5	2000m	Good 3	2-01.30	7/2	131,000
Cyril Small	57	1200m	Good 3	1-09.90	11/2	130,000
Cyril Small	57	1400m	Good 3	1-24.30	9/4	65,000
Cyril Small	57	1600m	Firm 2	1-34.00R	2/5	65,000
Cyril Small	57	1800m	Firm 2	1-47.30R	1/5	65,000
Cyril Small	57	1400m	Firm 2	1-22.20R	4/9	98,500
Cyril Small	59	2000m	Firm 2	2-01.90	7/4	131,000
Peter Cook	61	1400m	Firm 2	1-23.10	9/4	28,000
Cyril Small	61	1600m	Firm 2	1-35.30	4/7	33,000
Cyril Small	58.5	1800m	Firm 2	1-47.58	4/9	210,000
Cyril Small	57.5	1400m	Firm 2	1-23.30	1/4	65,000
Cyril Small	57.5	1600m	Firm 2	1-35.90	1/7	82,250
Cyril Small	58	1800m	Good 3	1-48.00	1/7	65,000
Cyril Small	58	2000m	Good 3	2-01.60	8/13	326,000
Cyril Small	59	1010m	Good 3	0-58.00	8/11	8,500
Cyril Small	58.5	1600m	Firm 2	1-35.40	10/9	172,150
Cyril Small	57.5	1400m	Good 3	1-23.30	7/4	65,000
Cyril Small	58	2000m	Good 3	2-00.90	12/1	427,500

Source: Racing Australia database

PART II

THE STORY CONTINUES FOR SOME

CHAPTER 14

LIVING LIFE POST-VO ROGUE

I remember when legendary Brisbane race caller Wayne Wilson called his last race in 2010 in Brisbane on radio 4TAB. He spoke to his listeners about the saying, 'Don't be sad it's over, be happy it happened'. That saying relates well to Vo's retirement. Of course, we were all sad that Vo had retired but ever so happy for the ride of a lifetime he took us all on and the thrills he gave us. Vo coming into our lives was like the gift that kept on giving, and I'm not just talking about the financial rewards. The experiences we had, the places we went, the people we met and the memories we treasure to this day. Our family could not have loved Vo any more if we had owned him ourselves.

Vo retired to Jeff's Tallebudgera Valley property. We visited regularly and on Vo's tenth birthday we ordered a beautiful cake we took down for him (well, it was for us really) to celebrate his special day. It was a carrot cake of course, with tiny carrots made from icing sugar decorated around the outside. Vo got real carrots.

The kids used to love riding on Vo's back; it was nothing for Vo to have Cymone, her brothers Steven and Mitchell, and our boys Daniel and Braidon sitting on him and all smiling for the camera with Jeff or Cyril holding onto the lead. Vo created a track around his yard.

He used to get quite a speed up as he would make his way around it. If you were standing on his track when he was wanting to work around—well, let's just say you had to get out of the way, because Vo wasn't stopping for anyone. The kids weren't on his back when he did that though, no one was, he just loved to work around.

But life goes on and while Vo had retired and was living the idyllic life, Cyril and Vic certainly hadn't retired, and despite Cyril's very quiet disposition, life was rarely dull.

On 30 July 1991 our second child, Braidon Robert was born. Cyril was riding at Ipswich that day and had ridden a winner when the Royal Brisbane Hospital put through a call to the stewards to tell them that if Cyril wanted to be with his wife when his baby was born, he better get moving. The stewards released Cyril from his other rides and he arrived just in time to welcome our gorgeous boy. Braidon is very independent and strongminded, and like Daniel and his father, he is an excellent horseman.

The following week, on 9 August, Cyril had seven rides at Beaudesert. A horse he was riding for Reg McKay, Modern Asset, bucked all the way from the barriers to the home turn where it eventually got rid of Cyril. Cyril was furious and had nothing nice to say to Reg about his horse. Cyril had ridden for Reg for years and continued to do so for some time after. Cyril injured his achilles heel when he fell and while he could put little weight on his foot, he could still ride. The trainers assisted him out to the horses and threw him on. He's a tough bugger and he went on to ride a winning treble that day.

Cyril's eventful day became even more so. A fellow in the crowd who Cyril didn't recognise, took great offence at Cyril's accomplishments. He told anybody that would listen that Cyril and Vic were the mafia, and he went on a right royal rant about that. Fortunately for that fellow, Vic wasn't in attendance. The police stepped in and escorted him from the track.

At that time, we had Ron Johnson staying with us assisting Cyril with his weight loss program. Ron had made a name for himself assisting jockeys to lose weight using his brown rice diet and body strengthening exercises. Cyril had three rides the next day at the Gold Coast and he was in quite a lot of pain by the time he got home. Ron went to the Clayfield markets and came back with ginger and other things and had Cyril in the bathroom transferring his foot from iced water to hot water. I think Ron may have put the ginger in the hot water but I can't be sure about that. Anyway, the purpose was to bring out the bruising and support a quicker recovery.

Cyril was in doubt about his ability to back up the next day so he gave his good mate Shane Scriven a call and told him what had happened. Shane was booked to ride at the Gold Coast as well. He had three rides also but in different races to Cyril. Shane told Cyril that he was in bed with the flu and not likely to get out of bed any time soon. They both agreed that whoever was in the best health the next day would take the rides. As it turned out Cyril took all six rides and the trainers assisted him to the horses and legged him on. He finished the day with a winner and a third placing. The winner, Minefield, was to have been one of Shane's rides for Ronnie and Mary Dillon, also long-time clients of Cyril.

At the very beginning of the 1991/92 racing season, Cyril's friend and long-time client Johnny Fitzgerald (Fitzi) approached Cyril to ride his two-year-old colt Luau Lover that he trained for Gail Parr. Gail had wanted Chris Munce to ride the horse but each time Fitzi asked Chris to come and ride the horse trackwork, Chris was unavailable with obligations to other trainers and their horses. Fitzi told Cyril that Gail was a very loyal person and should he work with the horse, Gail would stick with him. Cyril was happy to ride the young colt for Fitzi and Gail, and together they won a heat of the two-year-old trials.

Back then, the first two city two-year-old races were the JF Meynick Stakes for the colts and geldings, and the CE McDougall Stakes for the fillies, both Listed races run over 1000 metres at Eagle Farm. To be eligible to gain a start in those races, the youngsters had to trial and earn their place in the field. Cyril was also riding another promising young horse called Spoiling for trainer Peter Blackwell. Spoiling had won his trial just as impressively as Luau Lover. He too was entered for the Meynick Stakes but the owners had put him up for sale.

Everyone had an opinion about which horse Cyril should ride in the Meynick, including Race Club administrators. The majority told Cyril he should ride Spoiling, with many whispers around that Luau Lover was shin sore. Cyril's brother Warren and I told him he should ride Luau Lover. I'm not sure what Warren's reasoning was, but Fitzi had made it clear that as Gail was loyal, she expected the loyalty would be returned. If Cyril rode Spoiling, not only would he lose the future rides on Luau Lover, with Spoiling for sale, Cyril might not get to sit on him ever again either. So, he could find himself a two-time loser.

As the time came for Cyril to make a decision, the whispers became louder that Luau Lover was shin sore. Cyril popped into Fitzi's stables while Fitzi was there and walked into Luau Lover's box. He took a good long look at the horse then tested his legs for shin soreness. They were clean and pain free. So much for the whispers. Important information like that needs to come straight from the horse's mouth, so to speak, and it pretty well did. Luau Lover told Cyril exactly what he needed to know to make an informed decision.

Cyril and Luau Lover went on to win the Meynick Stakes. Spoiling finished fourth and was sold to high profile property developer David Devine who handed the horse to Kelso Wood to train. Cyril rode him a few times before being replaced by Gavan Duffy. Cyril and Luau Lover won another feature two-year-old race at Doomben in the March of '92. Cyril always had and still has a terrific affinity with two-year-olds.

By the September of '92, Cyril had forged a successful relationship with Killarney trainer Les Clarke. Les booked Cyril to ride his handy sprinter Untamed in the Lismore Quality Handicap, the feature sprint race of the two-day Lismore Racing Carnival. Untamed was a grey horse that Cyril had a lot of time for. Untamed's main opposition was champion country sprinter Tiny's Finito, the odds-on favourite for the race. Tiny's, as we all knew him, was trained at Glen Innes by Walter Doolan. His regular jockey was John Hutchings and going into the race Tiny's had 36 wins under his belt, including numerous wins at Listed level. He was also a Group 3 winner and was Group 1 and Group 2 placed. In fact, Tiny's beat Vo by just under two and a half lengths in the Listed Doomben Stakes during the Summer Carnival of 1990.

Untamed's resume paled into insignificance next to Tiny's, with eight wins to his credit, the best of those being a one metropolitan win race at a mid-week Canterbury meeting almost 10 months earlier. Even so, Cyril was quietly confident. Importantly, Untamed was only carrying 52.5kg while Tiny's had to lump 59.5kg. As they say in racing, weight can stop a train.

Back then, it was about a three-hour drive from Hendra to Lismore via the back roads. Cyril always took the back roads. He had driven them more often than not when driving from Brisbane to Bob's farm at Wyan.

We got just north of Kyogle when we hit a council roadworks sign. We found ourselves in a line of stopped traffic. Cyril got out of the car and walked up to the council workers. He could see that they had pulled the bridge across the creek down, and he asked the workers what they were doing. They told him they were repairing the bridge and if he waited an hour or so they would have a temporary crossing in place, otherwise he could take an alternate route that would add two hours to the journey. It was after 2pm and the race was at 4.20pm. Cyril had to be at the track by 3.20pm so neither option was suitable.

Cyril told the council workers he had a gun ride in the main race at Lismore and if they could just put two planks across the creek that would allow him to drive across, he would bring them a carton of beer on his way home. The council workers obliged, Cyril took the order for the beer, agreed to meet them at one of the pubs in the main street in Kyogle later in the day, and we went on our way.

Untamed bolted in by three lengths and smashed the track record by 0.8 seconds. Weight got the better of Tiny's and he finished fifth, almost five lengths behind Untamed.

The council workers were delighted when Cyril walked into the pub with their carton of beer. Cyril returned to Lismore the next day and won one of the feature support races to the Lismore Cup on the Peter Gardner-trained Margin. Untamed won three Lismore Quality Handicaps in a row—Cyril won on him in '92 and '94, and champion Northern Rivers jockey Graeme Birney won that race on him in '93. Today, the Lismore Quality has been renamed the Untamed Showcase Sprint.

* * *

While Cyril was going about his business doing his own thing, Vic was also busy doing his. It didn't take Vic too long to find another good horse in Quegent. While not in Vo's league, Quegent was a very handy horse all the same and Vic owned the horse with his brother Billy and Billy's close friend. Cyril still rode for Vic from time to time, including scoring three wins on No Sacrifice for him across the July/August of '93 at the Gold Coast and Caloundra. Vic had a lot of horses and he needed a capable rider who would be available to help him work his team, and that rider was a lovely young man named Jeff Wilson.

Jeff rode a lot of trackwork for Vic and was rewarded with many race rides. Jeff was a valuable asset to Vic's stable and together they had a lot of success on the country and provincial circuits.

'We had a lot of horses and Vic would get up at 2 o'clock in the morning and work horses down beside the airport,' recalls Jeff. 'I used to get up between 3.00am and 3.30am and meet him at the track at 4am as soon as the gates opened. I'd ride for him all morning and then depending on what time we finished, I would go and ride trackwork for other people. But he was a good bloke. We were great friends. Every now and again he would be edgy or cranky if I was late or the way I was riding or whatever, but apart from that he was always really funny, and I found him a good bloke.'

In the September of '92, Jeff Wilson was pretty stiff not to have ridden Quegent to win the VRC Ascot Vale Stakes. 'Vic was in Melbourne and was just about to call me to come down and ride Quegent when Steven King's manager rang and told him Steven would like to ride the horse. Vic put Steven on and I was left to watch the horse win on TV from the Gold Coast jockeys' room,' Jeff recalls.

Vic later provided Jeff with an opportunity in the Listed Craven Plate at Randwick on stayer Huamino. 'Unfortunately, the horse was sore and he ran last,' Jeff says. 'I went back to Sydney a few weeks later and ran fourth on him at Randwick in a lower grade race.'

* * *

The next two years we all went about living our lives. We experienced deep sadness, but we also experienced enormous joy. Sadly, on ANZAC Day eve 1993, Cyril's father Bob passed away. Cyril loved his father very much and Bob was truly one of the most beautiful people you could ever meet. Cyril and Bob were a lot alike: astute, excellent horsemen and very quiet.

On 25 January 1994 our third and youngest child, the very beautiful, intelligent and kind Jessica Jade Amelia Small was born and our family was complete. While Jess didn't forge a career with horses, just quietly, when they were kids, she could outride Daniel and Braidon all day long.

In the April of '94, as the first anniversary of Bob's passing drew closer, the family decided that the best way to remember Bob would be to hold a memorial race in his honour each year at the Casino Race Club. Soon after, the Bob Small Bridle came to fruition.

Two months prior to Bob's passing I bought a horse from him called Good Memory. His stable name was Bobby. Warren trained him and he had already completed a preparation without racing. I syndicated the horse into six shares and retained the managing share. Good Memory was showing promise in his trackwork but not putting it together in his races. I suggested to Warren that he nominate Good Memory for his father's race, a maiden event run on 20 April that year.

Bob's family and friends came from far and wide to the Casino races that day. The races were also televised via Sky Chanel so that was a coup for the Club. Good Memory did us all proud and with Cyril riding and wearing his father's racing colours, he raced away to win by five lengths.

Despite Cyril's extraordinary success on one of the greatest racehorses to ever grace the Australian turf, winning his father's race that day wearing his father's racing colours on the last horse his father bred, trained by his brother and part-owned by his wife, was one of the most satisfying days of his career.

CHAPTER 15

THE HENDRA VIRUS CLAIMS VIC'S LIFE

In September 1994, the racing industry in Brisbane would suffer perhaps the cruellest blow in its long and rich history. It was the month that the now infamous Hendra virus struck Vic's Victory Lodge stable. Coincidentally, what was now Victory Lodge was formerly Jim Marshall's home and stable property where Cyril lived as he completed his apprenticeship.

I remember that timeframe in that September so well, but not with any fondness. Cyril's brother Warren called on the evening of Wednesday 21 September to speak to him. Cyril had ridden that day at Lismore and hadn't returned home at the time Warren called. I remember saying to him, 'So what's news Waz?' Warren told me there were reports that Vic was very sick in hospital.

'That can't be true,' I said to him. 'I was speaking to Vic last week about Cyril riding a few horses for him.'

Warren again said that Vic was very sick and added that he might not pull through. I hung up the phone and called Cyril's mobile. I told him what Warren had said and Cyril said he would stop in at Vic's before coming home. When Cyril got home he told me that he had spoken with Lisa Symons, Vic's stable worker and friend, and Warren was correct, Vic was very sick and he was in hospital. I told Cyril he needed to go and visit Vic, and Cyril told me that Lisa said that there was no point. Vic wouldn't recognise him, he was not at all well.

Soon after, we heard that the horses at Vic's stables had some kind of neurological disorder. The horses were running around in their stables and running head on into their concrete stable walls. Horrific stories were being told by those close to the action but before long, the grizzly scenes were being telecast across Australia and probably to the rest of the world as well.

I remember watching the news in absolute disbelief. Autopsies were being conducted on-site at Vic's stables on horses that only days earlier were fit and healthy athletes. The news telecast showed people wearing full protection suits hosing down the street gutters in Williams Avenue that had filled with blood from the autopsies, and headless horse carcases were being lifted into trucks parked on the street in front of Vic's stables.

With Vic so sick in hospital, Lisa and Dr Peter Reid were left to deal with the utter nightmare that was unfolding at the stable complex. Peter was the attending vet who was charged with treating the horses and he called in the Department of Primary Industries. Cyril and I had known Peter for many years and he is an exceptional vet and a lovely, kind man. I remember Fitzi telling me at the time that he has never seen fear in anyone's eyes like the fear he saw in Peter's when the Hendra virus saga was taking place. Very quickly, the Queensland Government stopped the movement of all horses into and out of Hendra. Owners and trainers were desperate to get their horses out, with some moving them in the dead of night.

In late October 1995, the ABC *Background Briefing* program broadcast an interview with journalist Helen Thomas and key people who were at the stables during that time. The broadcast was titled 'Outbreak at Victory Lodge'. The interview transcript is available online if you Google it. In that interview, Peter told Ms Thomas, 'Seeing the way the horses were dying was absolutely terrifying.'

Jeff Wilson and his girlfriend at the time often visited Vic at his property. Jeff knew that Vic had at least one sick horse at the stables because he was there with Vic when Vic first started caring for it. However, Jeff could not have contemplated the fallout from that first horse's illness. Jeff came to hear that more horses had fallen ill and then Lisa told him that Vic was in hospital. Shortly after that, Jeff and his girlfriend visited Vic in hospital.

'Vic was in a room on his own and he was hooked up to a drip in his hand. He was a bit disoriented, but he didn't seem to be too bad. Vic was unaware about what was going on back at his stables. No one told him what was going on, because I think by then Quegent had died and if he had have known that Quegent had died that would have shattered him,' Jeff Wilson recalls. 'We just had chit chat asking him how he was, how he was feeling. He was saying he was crook, but he thought he'd recover and be able to go back to the stables. We didn't know he was that crook. We knew he was crook, but we didn't think it was serious enough to take his life. We planned on going back and visiting him again and then shortly after that we found out that he had passed away.'

Vic passed away on 27 September 1994. Early on the day of Vic's passing, before the news of his death was announced, we headed to Noosa to catch up with very dear friends of mine who I was close to all through my high school years. As the news of Vic's passing filtered out, Cyril's phone rang off the hook. Everyone in the media wanted to speak to him about Vic. Cyril had radio stations, television stations and the print media calling him all day. Eventually Cyril caught up with Channel Nine news at the Noosa Surf Club for an in-person interview.

Meanwhile, along with other stable staff, Jeff was interviewed by federal police who at first suspected Vic had been poisoned.

'I was picked up by a police car and taken to police headquarters in Brisbane where I was interviewed for about an hour and a half about Vic's health and how he died,' says Jeff. 'But Vic was unorthodox in his ways,' Jeff continued.

With the first of the sick horses lying on the ground, Jeff recalled Vic sitting beside it and clearing the muck from its nose. 'Vic had cuts on his hands and I have always believed that he contracted the virus through those cuts because of his close contact with this horse. Vic didn't wear protective gloves,' Jeff adds.

The day after Vic passed away Dr Gerry Murphy, who was at the time the Director of Public Health, held a press conference to discuss Vic's death in relation to the deaths of the horses. *The Courier Mail* newspaper reported Dr Murphy as having said, 'We have not excluded a link with the horses, but it is most unlikely.'

It is documented that Vic had suffered from Ross River virus and Hepatitis A prior to becoming sick with the respiratory illness that ultimately claimed his life. I have been told that officially the cause of his death is unknown; whether that is correct or not, I couldn't tell you for sure.

It would later be recorded that Vic was the first person in the world to die from what was initially called equine morbillivirus. The name of the virus was later changed to Hendra virus. As it turned out, the authorities believe that the virus was brought into Vic's stable from a horse, a mare called Drama Series, that had been spelling out at Cannon Hill, a southern suburb of Brisbane. In that spelling paddock was one or more trees that had bats in it.

It has since been found that bats that carry Hendra virus shed the virus through their urine, faeces or saliva. Horses can become exposed to those secretions by grazing under roosting sites. The virus is highly contagious and fatal to horses. It can be readily transmitted to humans via bodily fluids such as saliva and nasal congestion and is more often than not, fatal to the human population. One of Vic's stable staff, Ray Unwin, who also cared for the sick horses, also contracted Hendra virus at the same time as Vic, but fortunately Ray recovered.

Fourteen horses in Vic's stable died as a direct consequence of the Hendra virus, while six other horses were humanely euthanised because they carried the antibodies of the virus and it was feared that the virus could flare up inside them and become transmittable. Some of the horses that carried the antibodies were from an adjoining stable complex and belonged to a friend of ours. She and her husband were outstanding contributors to racing in Queensland and they loved their horses like they were family. They had purchased a lovely property near Fernvale where the horses could spell and live upon retirement. They never got over losing their horses in such a tragic way and unfortunately, they chose to leave the racing industry. It was a truly devastating period in many people's lives and especially for Vic's family and friends, the stable staff who had taken care of the horses and of course the owners of all the horses that died.

Vic had a catholic funeral that was well attended. I really don't remember a great deal more about that. What I do remember so clearly was attending the wake later that day at Fitzi's place. People from all walks of racing life were there. Cyril wanted to go to the bottle shop on Nudgee Road which was a short walk from Fitzi's. On the way back, Cyril just stopped walking, put his drinks down and hugged me crying and trembling. The enormity of the past weeks coupled with Vic's passing and how Cyril really felt about that had finally hit him. He was truly shattered.

Remembering Vic

In *The Age* newspaper on 7 March 1988, Les Carlyon wrote:

> Vic ... is now a confidant of premiers, knights of the realm, Toorak hostesses, as well as the hero of every battler who each morning slips a bridle over the ears of a cheap horse and tells the feed man the cheque is in the mail.

Vic achieved an enormous amount in his 49 short years, but it never changed him. He was an eccentric but likeable larrikin who could hold court like few trainers before him, or since for that matter. I personally believe that the world is a less interesting place without him in it. He deserved to be sitting on his veranda in later years telling yarns to his visitors about how he and his great horse Vo Rogue made the bluest bloods of thoroughbred horse racing owned by the extraordinarily wealthy look second rate. Vic would have been a sell out every time on the public speaking circuit. In fact, he did do a number of guest speaking appearances and each time he had the audience and the compere in stitches. He had so many stories to tell and incredibly, they were all true. I once came across a website that stated, 'Vic Rail became so famous that they named the whole Victorian railway network after him!' Of course, that's not true, but it makes for a great story.

Jeff Wilson concurs with Jeff Perry that Vic was very good at getting horses fit. 'Oh I remember the way we used to have to work the horses,' says Jeff Wilson. 'There would be times when Vic would get you to canter that slow you could honestly walk faster than he would have you canter the horse. I mean, he used to get horses that fit, and you would have to go around the sand track in the middle of Doomben probably about 10 or 12 times and he would want you to walk them off the track. No matter what, you were never allowed to trot, you were never allowed to canter, you'd have to walk off the track, no matter what. It would take nearly half an hour to three quarters of an hour to work one horse on a slow morning. Unbelievable!'

In remembering Vic as a horse trainer, Jeff Perry recalls, 'What I found with Vicky was if you listened to him when he talked, he would make sense. What he said about horses and training them, it made a lot of sense. What Vicky didn't have was the ability to put his words together. If he'd have gone to university and could learn to talk like Bob Hawke, now Hawke could talk for 45 minutes and say nothing. Vicky would talk and everybody wanted to take the piss and pick handles out of him, you know what I mean? But if you listened to him, he would explain it to you why things were being done that way. That's one thing I will say for Vicky, he was very thorough.'

Debby Osborne agrees with Jeff Perry and says, 'A lot of people used to take Vic as a fool because he was a bit rough in his mannerisms and the way he talked, he was not a highly educated man in schooling, but he was actually a very smart man. If you listened to him there was a reason for everything he did.'

Debby and Vic drifted apart in 1992, and Debby moved on to find her own way in life. Debby remembers Vic as, 'Probably still one of the best horsemen I have seen in my life. He could fix any horse; he could ride anything. There wasn't a horse that he could not ride—hard pullers or crazy horses, he could ride them.' Debby continues, 'Vic taught me so much. I could ride horses that the boys couldn't ride. I wouldn't be as good a horseperson as I am if it wasn't for Vic. As a jockey I was ordinary, but as a trackwork rider or horseperson I think I did okay. I owe everything I know to Vic. I've seen a lot of good horsemen and a lot of trainers, but he was probably the best I've seen.'

'And that's another thing,' Debby adds, 'Vic was a very good farrier. Vic would assist other farriers to gain better outcomes for horses if they were unsuccessful in gaining an outcome themselves. Vic could also do horses' teeth and Vic and I would also clip horses for other trainers.' Debby goes on to say that, 'Vic spent a lot of time with many different trainers over the years but he said he learned more from Tommy Woodcock in the first three months than he did in all the years he worked for other people.'

Vic attributed his success as a trainer to Tommy Woodcock. Vic worked for Tommy for five years, and Vic would often say that Tommy was the most genuine person he'd ever known and that the key things Tommy taught him were to keep his horses as close to nature as possible, feed them right and to use common sense.

Vic was a man of simple tastes. He loved horse racing, his horses and the punt, including the casino. He was as bad a gambler as he was a good one, and over the years he had more money go through his hands from punting than some people would earn in multiple lifetimes. Despite his newfound fame and wealth as the trainer of Vo Rogue, he didn't gain a taste for extravagant things and his favourite foods remained steak and veggies, fish and chips, and ice cream. I remember after Vo won his first race in Melbourne, we went to dinner later that night at a steak and pizza place.

Vic looked through the menu and called the waitress over, 'Lovey,' Vic said, 'I just want plain steak and vegetables, none of this other stuff. Do you think I can order that? Just plain steak and vegetables?'

Vic was also a non-drinker. He would tell you himself he didn't need to drink alcohol, he was mad enough as it was, he didn't need any help. I'm just repeating what Vic would say.

Vic was never worried by what others might think. He did things his way. Debby tells me of the night that Vic attended the Albion Park trots and when he attempted to put his car into gear to drive home, the only gear that would work was reverse. So, Vic drove his car home in reverse from Albion Park to Hendra. I'm not sure if it was good luck or good management—although I suspect good luck—that the police did not pull Vic over that night. With all the CCTVs following our every move in this day and age, I can only imagine that had they been installed back then, for anyone watching Vic driving past one CCTV then another it would have been a WTF moment.

Vic also made headline news in Melbourne one year when he punched a taxi driver because Vic thought the taxi driver had taken him the long way round to increase the cost of the fare. Vic had a very different take on money to most people. Jeff Wilson also suggests to me that to some extent, Vic was frugal. Maybe—or perhaps he just put different values on different things. He wasn't big on paying bills, he didn't see that as a priority. He wasn't interested in investments that were not related to gambling, and he thought the cost of food was ridiculous.

Jeff Wilson tells the story of Vic having a crack at a lady in the bistro at the Toowoomba races who sold him a hotdog for $1.20. Jeff recalls Vic saying to her, 'I can't believe you're gonna charge $1.20

just for that sausage.' Jeff adds, 'He did end up buying it and put it in his pocket for later on. But yet he could put $1000 or even $15000 on a racehorse, watch it get beat and he wouldn't blink an eyelid. It wouldn't phase him.'

Jeff Perry agrees with Jell Wilson's assessment and said, 'Well that's exactly right, well we all know that. But that was his life you know.'

Vic was a firm believer in the adage that one man's trash is another man's treasure, he had a real penchant for a bargain. One of my favourite personal memories of Vic revolves around my pair of black leather pants and Vic's new trousers. The year was 1989 and Cyril and I had been to the Queen Victoria Market a few times. Back then leather was the in thing, particularly black leather pants. All the ladies were wearing them, but they were quite expensive. I had spotted a pair that were $125, and back then, that was a lot of money to pay for a pair of pants. Cyril told me that if Vo won the Australian Cup he would buy those leather pants for me, which he did.

One day soon after, I was wearing them in Vic's company. Vic commented to me that he liked my leather pants. He then said to me, 'What do you think about the trousers I'm wearing?' He then took my hand and he put my hand on his lower leg and said, 'feel the quality of the material, just beautiful.'

And I said, 'Yeah terrific Vic, they're great.'

And then he said to me, '$2 from Vinnies, and I liked them so much I bought two pairs.' I thought that was gold.

To top it off, as Vic's suit shirts got a little bit tight around the neck, he didn't see any need to let an otherwise good shirt go to waste. Vic creatively placed a safety pin through the top buttonhole and covered it with a tie. No one was any the wiser and it was the perfect solution.

I have met many people who knew Vic well and they all have their own stories about him to tell. But there is no doubt, none of us have met anyone quite like Vic. He was one of a kind.

Another tragedy befalls the stable

Just over one year following Vic's death, the hand of fate stepped in and dealt Vic's loyal young friend and former stable jockey the worst card of his life. On the morning of 10 October 1995, then 25-year-old Jeff Wilson headed to the barrier trials at Eagle Farm. A horse Jeff rode that morning jumped from the outside barrier and ran away from the horses on its inside and ran into the outside running rail. On impact, the saddle slipped and Jeff was propelled into the steel upright which shattered his spine. Jeff was left a paraplegic with his life spent confined to a wheelchair.

In 2007, I interviewed Jeff Wilson and wrote an article about him for my friend Phil Purser's Just Racing website. The article was reproduced in the *Racing Queensland* magazine. In that interview, Jeff told me that his recovery to the point of leaving hospital some five and a half months later was long and painful, both physically and mentally. Jeff said that the most harrowing effect the injury had on him was bouts of severe depression. He attempted to take his own life on no less than three occasions.

'It's not just the fact that you can't walk, it is all the behind-the-scenes problems that no one can see,' said Jeff. 'The constant bladder infections, pressure sores, drinking water all the time, having to sleep on special pressure-relieving sheepskins on your bed, sitting on a special $700 cushion to relieve pressure sores. Every morning when I am trying to get dressed, I have a stressful moment and at times it can become unbearable. The effort to get dressed can be unbelievable.'

It took Jeff many, many years to come to terms with his injury and his new life. I am happy to say that Jeff can now drive a car and he is mentally in a far better place and leading a happier life.

Vic Rail
(1945 – 1994)

To think I did all that
And may I say, not in a shy way
Oh, no, oh, no, not me
I did it my way

Frank Sinatra, 1969

Photo: Noel Pascoe

CHAPTER 16

CYRIL'S BAD FALL

I lost my Dad on 18 January 1995, one week before Jessie's first birthday and 10 days before my thirtieth. It was a crushing blow for me as we were very close. In January 1999 on Magic Millions day, we moved our family to the Gold Coast. The kids had outgrown our suburban property at Hendra that backed onto the back straight of Doomben racecourse. I was forever calling the racecourse manager Warren Williams to tell him there was a tennis ball, cricket ball, football, etc, on the course proper at the 1200-metre mark.

The kids always loved visiting their uncles, aunties and cousins on their expansive farms in Wyan and they all loved horses and wanted one of their own. After a search that took us far and wide, Jeff found us a 7.5 acre block in Tallebudgera Valley, not far from his family and Vo. We rented while my brother Raoul built our house, which we moved into in April 2000.

The family had settled into Gold Coast life just fine. We each had our own horse and loved going on family rides. The kids were in a great school, I was at university studying an MBA degree, and Cyril's career was rocking along nicely. He had formed an excellent association with Coominya trainer Lynn Paton who had successfully made the transition from the harness racing code to the thoroughbreds. Cyril and Lynn won a lot of races across South East Queensland with tried horses Lynn had purchased from other stables.

In the September of 2002, Lynn and her then-husband Peter took two truckloads of horses out to Birdsville for the two-day carnival. Cyril flew out to ride them courtesy of Craig Black who found him a seat on a six-seater plane. Cyril rode in every race across the two days and came away with two winners, a second and a third.

Six weeks later, we had family visiting who wanted to see Vo. We took them up to Jeff's and Cyril gave Vo a good pat. Later that day, Cyril was riding at Eagle Farm for Lynn on her horse Regulations, who was Group 3 placed and a Listed winner in Sydney when trained by Bryan Guy. I suggested to Cyril that he didn't wash the hand that patted Vo and when he got legged up on Regulations, that he run his hand all over his neck for good luck. Cyril did that and Regulations won. The winning margin was a neck.

The following week, Saturday 26 October 2002 started no differently to any other Saturday. Cyril kissed me goodbye as he left for the Gold Coast races and asked me what I would be doing for the day. The kids had a friend over and I was studying for exams. I was almost halfway through my MBA degree at that time. Cyril had had a few too many race falls and injuries in the previous six years, and I worried about what the future would hold for our family should he suffer a career-ending injury. I decided that I better get myself well-educated so I could get a good job and take the reins as the money-maker if necessary.

At 1.32pm that afternoon, I came within a whisker of realising my worst fears. Cyril was riding a four-year-old gelding called Kings Cross in Race 2 for trainer Trevor Fay. It was a maiden race for colts, geldings and entires. The horse had previously been trained in Broadmeadow and after 10 race starts that resulted in one second and one third, the horse was sold to clients of Trevor. Cyril had ridden the horse in trackwork prior to the race. Approaching the 600 metres, the horse fell and speared Cyril headfirst into the track. Kim Bell riding Teltime crashed over the top of him.

Cyril lay on the track for about 45 minutes; he was unconscious for three or four of those and there was real concern about his condition. The paramedics at the Turf Club were extra careful in moving him.

Cyril was initially taken to Pindara Hospital located close to the Gold Coast Turf Club. I went straight to the hospital, taking the kids and their friend with me. I had them stay in the waiting room while I went into the emergency department (ED) to see Cyril.

At that time I was not aware that Cyril had been unconscious or of the concerns that the paramedics had for him at the track. He was wearing a neck brace and seemed in good spirits—not overly worried about himself.

There were a few x-rays and other examinations that needed to be done so while they did that, the kids and I went over to the Turf Club so I could pick up Cyril's race gear and other belongings. On the way out, I stopped to watch Northerly win the second of his two Cox Plates on the racecourse TV.

When I returned to the ED, I noticed that Cyril's neck brace had been removed. I said to him, 'Your neck brace has been removed. That's good. Obviously you don't have a broken neck.' No sooner did I get those words out of my mouth, a doctor raced into the room and said that the x-ray hadn't picked up the breaks, but the MRI had. Suddenly, things went from no worries to lots of worries. The doctor called in a nurse and instructed her to carefully fit a neck brace.

The MRI revealed that Cyril had three fractures in his neck including an unstable fracture of the C2, also known as the hangman's fracture. Cyril required specialist care and was transferred to the Allamanda Private Hospital. By the time he got settled in his condition worsened. A doctor was stationed in his room for the first 24 hours.

As I left him that Saturday evening Cyril said to me, 'Call Lenny [Hill], ask him to call Mick [Dittman] and have him arrange for Maureen's doctor to look after me.'

Maureen Dittman had been diagnosed some years earlier with a brain tumour. She was full of praise for her neurosurgeon for whom she attributed at that time to her still being alive. A leading neurosurgeon had been appointed to look after Cyril but he only wanted Maureen's doctor.

I managed to drift off to sleep late on Saturday night only to wake up in the early hours of Sunday morning. I remember thinking what a terrible nightmare I had just woken from. I put my hand out to touch Cyril and make sure he was okay, only to realise that I hadn't woken from a nightmare at all. Cyril wasn't sleeping beside me, our daughter Jess was. She had climbed into bed to keep me company.

As the sun started to come up the phone rang. It was Shane Scriven. He was in Macau when the news had filtered out to him, and he wanted to know how Cyril was. I couldn't tell him a great deal, but I remember I cried a lot. I was very frightened for what the future held for Cyril and what that might mean for our family.

Further investigations found that Cyril had also sustained four fractured vertebrae in his back, a shell fracture of his entire facial structure and a broken nose. His condition was listed as critical but stable.

Mick appeared at Cyril's bedside on Sunday morning and the next day Maureen's neurosurgeon was appointed as Cyril's specialist.

Cyril was a very unwell man and he was confined to bed for the first week before the ward sister assisted Cyril in moving from the bed to a lounge chair in his room. It was a huge deal for Cyril and the sister gave him pethidine to help with the pain. Cyril's body started shaking uncontrollably and I was so worried about the effect the drug was having on him. The ward sister turned to me and said, 'we can always tell our patients who don't take drugs by the way their bodies react to these drugs.'

As he got stronger, Cyril started walking laps around the nurses' station and then around the ward. Cyril weighed 47kg when he was discharged some 18 days after the fall, and he had just one thing on his mind: riding again.

Two months after the accident when Cyril was on the mend, I asked the neurosurgeon why a doctor had been stationed in his room at the Allamanda for the first 24 hours after admission. He told me that there was concern that the unstable C2 fracture may shift with a build-up of pressure around the fracture site. I asked him what the doctor would have done had that happened. He said there was nothing the doctor could have done—had the fracture shifted, Cyril would have died.

It became clear to me that the first responders—the paramedics at the Gold Coast Turf Club—had saved Cyril's life. We never met those people but as a family we are forever indebted to them and forever grateful. I recall speaking to a journalist about Cyril's fall and telling him, 'Cyril knocked on heaven's door but nobody answered.' Cyril received cards and gifts from people across Australia, many he had never met. It was just so lovely that people would want to wish him well.

Cyril only has two gears: overdrive and stop. His recovery didn't change that.

Once he got the 'all clear' from his specialist to change from a hard neck collar to a soft neck collar, I had to strongly chastise him for riding the kids motorbike and doing wheelies across the paddock. Really!! Not to mention the day I was studying and looked out the window to see Cyril mowing a section of the paddock above the dam.

Our property is predominantly flat but we have a dam on it that is about 40-plus metres long and 10 metres across. On the house side of the dam is a dam wall. You cannot see into the dam from the house. The other side of the dam sits into a short but relatively steep hill that goes up to the fence line near the road. That section is about 12 metres. Cyril was mowing back and forth up and down the hill, rather than the other more dangerous option which is to mow across it. I walked across the paddock and said to him, 'Can you please stop mowing here? It's too steep and too dangerous. You'll finish in the dam.'

'I'll be right,' Cyril said to me. 'Go back inside and stop watching.'

I had only just got inside when our dog Banjo started barking madly. I looked out across the paddock and couldn't see Cyril. I ran across to the dam and there he was sitting on top of his submerged tractor. You seriously have to have nerves of steel to live with some people.

On 30 April 2003, Cyril's close friend, trainer Kevin Vizer passed away from leukemia. Kevie and Cyril were wonderful friends, and they had a lot of success on the racetrack together. To Cyril, Kevie, his wife Sandra and five kids were family. Kevie's passing really took the wind out of Cyril's sails for a while.

As Cyril's health improved, I felt torn. I had several people saying to me, 'you can't possibly let him ride again', while others were saying to me, 'you have to let him ride again'. I really didn't want Cyril to ride again, but as he got closer to a full recovery Cyril came to me and he said, 'I was a jockey when you met me. Being a jockey is who I am, it is what I do.'

Cyril resumed riding at Eagle Farm in the September of 2003, less than 11 months after the accident, and rode at the minimum riding weight of 53kg. His first winner back was for Lynn Paton at Beaudesert on 13 September on a horse called Quiet Smytzer.

CHAPTER 17

VO'S FINAL YEARS

Vic and Jeff never called their horse a champion, but everyone else did, including me. He was the first Queensland-trained horse to win $1,000,000 in prizemoney. He raced across six racing seasons, won across four States, and in an era filled with champions he broke five track records between the distances of 1400 metres and 2040 metres. He captured the imagination of racegoers Australia-wide and in doing so, achieved a cult-like following that exists to this very day.

On 23 August 2004 at the annual Queensland Racing Awards Night, Vo was inducted into the Queensland Racing Hall of Fame. He was 21 years old and loving life. Other nominees for the award included Dalrello, Falvelon, Fitzgrafton, Lough Neagh and Tails. A limousine was sent to our place to pick up Jeff, Cymone, Cyril and me and take us to the event that was held in the Grand Ballroom of The Sheraton in Brisbane. We were seated with legendary former champion jockey Darby McCarthy and his family. Darby was also inducted into the Hall of Fame that evening. It was a truly wonderful night but there was one person missing who deserved to share in the accolades and frivolities of the evening, and that person was Vic.

In 2008, Vo's health took a turn for the worse. He came down with laminitis. Contrary to popular belief, Vo did not live with us throughout his retirement years, he lived with Jeff for all but one year and that was the year he lived with us. The property that Jeff and Cymone were living in on Trees Road, Tallebudgera Valley was steep in many places. Vo was having difficulty getting around and his condition was not improving; rather, it was getting worse. Cyril suggested that Vo move to our property which is more suited to a horse with laminitis, and as the crow flies is basically on the other side of the mountain from where Vo lived.

Vo's arrival took precedence over all other horses. Initially we put him in a stable that allowed him to walk out into a small yard. Jeff was there every morning and every afternoon tending to Vo's every need. Cymone would accompany Jeff most times.

I vividly recall one morning Vo was very weak on his feet. It was more than an effort for him to stand and it took several minutes for him to walk from the stable into his yard which is about a five-metre walk. I tried to hold myself together and not cry as I looked at Jeff who was gently encouraging his best friend to keep going. I thought for sure Jeff would have to call it, and by that, I mean humanely put Vo down. Thank god I was wrong.

Jeff had every faith in his courageous and lion-hearted horse that he could rise to the occasion one more time and win the fight, this time for his life. Jeff bought special boots to support Vo's feet and when they didn't assist Vo, Jeff bought another pair of better special boots. Jeff also had a farrier attending to Vo regularly and Jeff threw literally everything at Vo to get him over the line.

Vo's health improved and we were able to move him to a paddock by the creek that has lovely shade trees in it. Vo loved that paddock; all the horses do.

In March of 2009, racing legend John Tapp OAM contacted Cyril and Jeff about doing an interview with them for his program *Inside Racing* on Sky Channel. It was arranged that John and his small crew would come out to our place one Sunday in the late morning. I was so excited that John was coming to our place. I have been a fan of John since I was a young girl and it is my opinion that he was the best race caller in the country when he was race calling. Prior to having the true honour of meeting John, he always came across as a highly knowledgeable and sincerely lovely gentleman, which I now know him to be. John is well versed in all things harness and thoroughbred racing. I wouldn't want to play a racing themed trivial pursuit game against him, but I sure would want to be on his team if such a game was played.

It was a stinking hot day when John and his crew came to tape the segment. Vo became terribly unwell quite quickly. It was unexpected. The camera crew came into the paddock to tape footage of Vo and at one point he was on the ground. Cyril put the hose on him to try and cool him down. I was so frightened that Vo would pass away with the cameras rolling. The cold water from the hose did the trick though and Vo got to his feet once more. When we were satisfied that Vo was happy and safe, we went inside and the interviews were taped.

Vo eventually made a full recovery from his laminitis which was really an extraordinary effort. No horse is entitled to shake off laminitis at the age of 25, and particularly having been so significantly sick. But as we all know, Vo was brave and determined and he was also surrounded by people who loved him first and foremost and pulled out all stops to save his life.

After a year with us, Vo returned to Jeff's care. Later, Jeff moved to Tamborine on the northern end of the Gold Coast. Jeff was very particular when choosing the property he placed Vo—it was of the utmost importance that the ground was kind to Vo's feet.

Vo's final years were spent in good health for a horse of his age, and Cyril would visit him from time to time. He always loved spending time with his champion, and I think Vo enjoyed the visits as much as Cyril did.

But unfortunately, death is inevitable for all of us.

For Vo, that day was 7 May 2012. It was a Monday, and the Labour Day holiday in Queensland. The day started out for us like any other autumn day on the beautiful Gold Coast. Cyril and I were looking forward to heading down to Burleigh Beach for a family and friends birthday lunch. Cyril was up at 3am and went to the track to put a dozen or so horses through their paces.

In 2008, I completed a Certificate IV in Racing (Owner/Trainer) with Racing Queensland and secured my thoroughbred trainer's licence. So, I too had been to trackwork as my home bred horse Millhousen was less than a week away from resuming from a long spell. Now at home, Cyril and I had fed and watered our small army of retired racehorses and had finally sat down for a coffee.

It was mid-morning when the phone rang. Cyril answered it on speaker phone. It was Jeff. He got straight to the point. 'Vo's down, I can't get him up,' he said. 'I'm going to have to put him down. Do you want me to wait and you can come up and say goodbye?'

There was a long pause before Cyril answered. 'No mate, I want to remember him as I do if that's all right?'

'Yeah, all right,' said Jeff.

Cyril hung up the phone, and we hugged each other as we cried. Our beautiful boy, who had been a massive part of our lives and our kids' lives, was gone. We were absolutely devastated and completely unprepared for it despite Vo's age. He was 28.5 years old. My thoughts turned to Jeff. He would be crushed.

The next morning at the track I was putting the work boots on Millhousen before legging Cyril on board. A large, sad figure appeared at the tie up stall. It was Jeff. Cyril shook his hand and said nothing. I stood up and wrapped my arms around Jeff with tears welling in my eyes.

'Are you okay?' I asked him.

'Yeah yeah, I'm alright,' Jeff replied unconvincingly. Of course he wasn't all right; none of us were.

For many in thoroughbred horse racing, even the best horses they are privileged to connect with, come and go from their lives. Vo was an exception. To us, he was as much a pet, and family member, as he was a champion racehorse.

Vo had a good life. No he didn't, he had a great life. He was much loved by Jeff, Cymone, all of our family, those that were close to him over the years including Vic, Debby, Vic's staff, and Garry Roberts, and of course the Australian racing public and the press. Jeff cared for Vo from when he bought him at the age of 11 months, to the day he died, aged 28 years and six months. Even in retirement, Vo came first with Jeff. He was totally devoted to his horse. As mournful as we were for losing our special boy, our hearts broke for Jeff because he lost his best friend.

Vo was the people's champion and Cyril thought they should know their hero had died. With Jeff's approval to release the news, Cyril called 'Miracle' Malcolm Johnston who was doing a sterling job as co-host of *Off The Rails* on Sky Channel. Before long, Vo's passing was known across Australia and many glowing tributes were given to the great horse.

On 10 May 2012, Matt Stewart for News Corp Australia, wrote:

Vo Rogue, the people's champion, dies at 28

VO Rogue, who died this week at the age of 28, dragged the sport of kings back to the commoners; ran the notion that bloodlines counted and aristocracy ruled into the ground …

… on song there was no more magnificent sight than front-running Vo Rogue at full gallop. The champions couldn't reel him in.

People would hang over fences when Vo Rogue ambled back to scale. They'd chuckle at the irony of this bare-footed, dusty-coated Queenslander, who dragged down the toffs and was the best horse in an era of champions.

CHAPTER 18

CARRYING ON THE TRADITION

People say that racing is in your blood. Our sons Daniel and Braidon would likely agree. While they didn't see their father ride Vo to so many thrilling and great victories, his achievements weren't lost on them. With their sister Jess, they grew up on racecourses across South East Queensland and the Northern Rivers. Most of their friends were from racing families, and they still are today.

Cyril wanted our boys to have every chance to be the very best riders and horsemen they could be. One day in late 2001 Cyril came home from the Ipswich races and he said to me, 'I've taken the boys as far as I can. I'm now handing them over to the best there is.'

'Who would that be?' I asked.

And Cyril replied, 'Bob Bayliss.'

Bob and Hazel Bayliss owned and operated Hilly Red Farm (also known by those close to them as 'The Lodge') at Ripley just south of Ipswich. The property was about 3000 acres in size and Bob and Hazel grew watermelons and pumpkins, mined sand, and bred and raised cattle, among other things. Bob was Clerk of the Course at Eagle Farm and Ipswich for 35 years. Bob and Hazel's son Jamie was a terrific jockey who won the 1989 Ipswich Cup on Dixie Kid. Jamie's sons Jake and Regan are also both top line jockeys today.

From January 2002, Daniel (then aged 12) and Braidon (then 10), spent one or more weeks of every school holidays for five years with Bob and Hazel at Hilly Red Farm. Bob taught them how to muster, dehorn, castrate and brand cattle. He taught them how to break in horses and importantly how to be an excellent 'pick up' person as Clerk of the Course—a role both boys would go on to do at the Gold Coast Turf Club. Both Daniel and Braidon are fine horsemen today due to the grounding their father gave them and the higher-level skills they learned from Bob. The boys see the Bayliss family as their own and they were crushed when Bob passed away in November 2020. Like their father, our boys have only ever had a working life with horses, mostly racehorses.

At the age of 15, while still at school at Marymount College, Daniel commenced riding trackwork. He also completed a Certificate III in Racing (Trackrider) as a part of a school-based traineeship through Racing Queensland, with champion trainer Alan Bailey. Daniel hitched a ride to the track with Cyril and rode trackwork from 4am to 8am each morning, before Cyril dropped him off to school on the way home. In Daniel's senior year at school, he was awarded the Vocational Excellence Award and was a Gold Coast regional finalist for the same award.

Braidon wasn't going to be left behind, and when he turned 15, he joined Cyril and Daniel in the car at stupid o'clock six mornings a week heading to the Gold Coast Turf Club to ride trackwork. He initially rode for Gary Newham and then moved to John Morrisey. Like Daniel, after trackwork Braidon was then dropped at school on Cyril's way home until Braidon decided, much to my disapproval that fell on deaf ears, that he would just leave school and work with horses.

After completing year 12, Daniel spent five or six years as a cast member of The Australian Outback Spectacular. He rode trackwork six mornings a week, and four or sometimes five nights a week he would work at the show from 3.30pm to after 10pm. They were long days and Daniel learned to sleep fast. He was in three different productions including *Spirit of the Horse with a Tribute to Phar Lap*. Daniel taught the other cast members how to 'race ride'. Daniel played numerous roles including a trick rider, farm hand, young Bluey, old Bluey, a jockey and Harry Telford, the trainer of Phar Lap.

Braidon's horse Centro, who raced as Il Centro Gold, also joined the cast in 2011. Evan Hartley gave Braidon the horse as a two-year-old in the May of 2000. Braidon had many fabulous adventures with Centro as they grew up together, and Centro spent seven years as a favourite among the human cast members of the Outback Spectacular. Centro learned how to jump over burning logs, line dance, be part of a roman riding team that requires a person to stand on the back of two horses as they canter around the arena, and he could jump into the back of a ute.

The one stipulation about Centro going to The Australian Outback Spectacular was that he came home to us upon his retirement, which he did. Centro is now 25 years young and at Pony Club teaching beginner riders how to compete in low level show jumping. He is a wonderful horse loved by everyone who meets him. Centro is one of the best examples of how talented, intelligent, versatile and adaptable thoroughbreds are, and what a wonderful life they can have if managed correctly.

* * *

Late in 2010, I was sitting in the grandstand at the Gold Coast Turf Club waiting for one of my horses, Leica Story, to participate in a jump out. Braidon came and sat with me. He had something very important to tell me. To give context to this part of the story, as a youngster Braidon had only ever wanted to be a jockey. When he was 10 years old he would dress up in a pair of his father's jockey breeches, put on a set of racing colours Mary Dillon had given us, and race Centro or

Bert (Rio Pelligrino) across the paddock. Braidon's favourite jockey was Glen Boss (Bossy) and Braidon would stand up in the irons and do the big salute that Bossy has become famous for.

Braidon was only 12 at the time Cyril recommenced riding after the fall that nearly took his life. Braidon went to every race meeting he could with his father for the next three years and he would carry Cyril's gear into the jockey's room and watch everything that happened. Having seen the battle his father had to endure to get his career back on track would have been enough to consider a career away from racing. But no, not Braidon. However, he grew a lot from the age of 14 and his prospects of becoming a jockey had all but diminished.

When Braidon was 17, family friend Paul Hamblin dropped in for a sleepover. Paul is a brilliant horseman and was a leading apprentice in the '80s. Weight got the better of him and he headed south to try his luck as a jumps jockey in Victoria. At the time he visited us, Paul had not long returned from riding in Europe and he brought with him a video of him race riding over the jumps. We all sat down to watch and Braidon was immediately hooked. Paul told him that if he ever decided he wanted to give it a go, Paul would help him.

So there we were, sitting in the grandstand at the Gold Coast Turf Club when Braidon delivered the news to me. He had made the decision to leave the Gold Coast and move to Warrnambool.

Paul had organised for him to work for Ciaron Maher and for Braidon's girlfriend Amy to work for Matthew Williams, who she would later become apprenticed to. At that time Braidon was 19, he had a well-paid job working for John Morrisey, he was living with Amy and Daniel one street from the beach at the southern end of Surfers Paradise, and he had his family and close friends around him.

He said to me, 'Mum, I don't want to be 30 years old and wonder if I would have been a good jumps jockey or not. I want to know at the age of 30 that I was good, or I wasn't.'

Despite my enormous sadness that Braidon was moving far, far away from us, I had the greatest respect for his decision. I said to him, 'Brady, most people in this world wouldn't take the risk you are taking to follow their dreams. You have so much security around you, yet you are not afraid to leave that behind and back yourself. I'm very proud of you.'

In the first week of January 2011, Braidon and Amy farewelled the Gold Coast and headed to Warrnambool.

* * *

Since 2011, Cyril and I have made regular trips to Victoria, and even to South Australia, to spend time with Braidon and his family, and to support Braidon in his jumps jockey career. We particularly love going to Warrnambool each year, or 'The Bool' as it is often called. It is such a fun time—it's like Schoolies for adults.

Braidon's first four rides were in highweight events—flat races with a higher weight scale that only those holding a jumps jockey's licence can ride in. We were at Murray Bridge in South Australia for Braidon's very first ride over the jumps, a steeplechase on Monday 11 June 2012 where he rode a horse called Big Jam for Jarrod McLean. He came last—excluding the horse that failed to finish—but that's okay, Braidon's career was underway.

We hired a car and drove the six hours from Murray Bridge to Warrnambool with Braidon and Paul Hamblin as passengers. Cyril and I spent a few days with Braidon and Amy before heading home prior to Braidon's next ride which was at Bendigo on Sunday 17 June.

We had Millhousen in at Caloundra that same day. Millhousen was having his third run back from a spell and ran out of his skin to finish third, only a neck from the winner. I was ecstatic with the run and while my strapper took care of the horse, I moved over to the TV screen to watch Braidon ride Jeune Baby Jeune for trainer Aaron Purcell. It was Braidon's first jumps ride in Victoria and his second jumps ride overall.

Braidon had previously finished second on Jeune Baby Jeune in a highweight race. He had educated this horse for jumps racing and ridden him in jumps trials. He thought the horse was going well enough for his debut and he gave himself and the horse a strong chance in the race. I was feeling quite confident for him and particularly happy for Small Racing and Millhousen's effort.

When the barriers opened, Jeune Baby Jeune took up a prominent position near the lead. He jumped the first two hurdles well. Coming into the straight the first time, Jeune Baby Jeune was leading. As they approached the jump the horse's attention was taken and he turned his head towards the outfield where the patrons can stand and watch the race. Braidon then straightened him and a few strides out from the jump he turned his head again towards the outfield and then took fright. He didn't try to jump the hurdle—instead, he ran sideways through the wing and ultimately through the inside running rail.

The horse stayed on its feet, but Braidon crashed to the ground. I was hysterical and immediately panicked. I watched as the horses continued on and as the horses came into the straight the second time, I caught sight of Braidon. He had got to his feet and dusted himself off. He sustained a greenstick fracture to his right hand I think it was, while the horse had skin off him and a cut to his eye. Both of them were very lucky and thankfully, Racing Victoria had replaced the timber running rails at their racetracks with collapsible running rails that are a much safer option.

Cyril and I taped that race and we watched it over and over again. The incident did not sit well with either of us. I spoke to one of Racing Victoria's senior stewards and told him that Cyril and I were of the belief that something in the outfield had frightened the horse.

To make our case stronger, an hour after the incident took place, a set of eight frame-by-frame photos of Braidon and Jeune Baby Jeune crashing through the wing and the inside running rail were uploaded to a website dedicated to denouncing horse racing. Amy sent me the photos and they were labelled with the website's name. Perhaps that something that frightened the horse was a camera flash. Another person suggested to me it could have been a laser. I would like to think that no one would be so malicious and despise horse racing so much that they would purposely put jockeys and their horses lives in danger by taking a laser to a racetrack and pointing it into the race field.

The senior steward took my call very seriously. He interviewed Braidon who couldn't help him—he had his eyes firmly set on the jump and keeping his horse's head straight. The steward looked through all the steward's video footage of the race but couldn't find anything. I didn't expect he would as the cameras are focused on the horses and the racetrack rather than the outfield. We were grateful for his time all the same. Cyril and I are of a firm belief as to what we think happened that day, but proving it is a whole different ballgame.

Braidon is tough like his father though. He didn't let the incident dent his passion or take away his dream to ride. The very next week at Casterton, Braidon rode his first winner, Telesmon, in a maiden hurdle event for trainer Matthew Williams. We cheered and I cried. It is a really tough gig being the mother of a jumps jockey. Telesmon was Braidon's only winner in his first season of riding but to be fair he started late in the season and only had six jumps rides.

He impressed those at the Australian Jumping Racing Association and was presented with the Encouragement Award at their annual dinner. Cyril and I flew down for the event which was held at Caulfield racecourse. It had been a long time since we had been to Caulfield. It holds many great memories for Cyril and that night a new great memory was added to the list. When Braidon's name was announced, his peers gave him a big round of applause. I think Braidon's tenacity and courage impressed them all. Cyril and I were so proud of him.

CHAPTER 19

OVERCOMING ADVERSITY

In 2015, Cyril and I went to the Hong Kong International Race Week in the second week of December. It rates up there as one of the best experiences of our lives. Cyril caught up with Zac Purton, who is a magnificent ambassador for not just Hong Kong racing but for racing on a global platform. After Breakfast with the Stars at Sha Tin racecourse, Zac took a group of people, including us, on an impromptu tour of the jockeys' room and the huge room where the racing colours are kept. Zac explained that in Hong Kong, each horse is allocated their own individual set of racing colours that their jockey wears when riding that particular horse. One set is held at Sha Tin racecourse and another set is held at Happy Valley racecourse. What a great idea! That works well for a racing precinct such as Hong Kong. In Australia, horses are assigned the racing colours belonging to their owners or trainer.

Just prior to leaving for Hong Kong, Jeff Perry told us he was having surgery on his left leg. He had a blockage in the knee and he was having the main vein replaced.

On Christmas Day, we called Jeff on speaker phone to wish him and Cymone Merry Christmas and to ask him if he was going to the Vo Rogue Plate at the Gold Coast Turf Club the next day. We were initially going to race my horse that I was training, Dubai Gee Eye, at Ballina on Boxing Day but the rain washed out the meeting. So instead, Cyril accepted an invitation from the Gold Coast Turf Club to present the winning trophies for the Vo Rogue Plate.

Jeff told us he was in hospital and things had not gone as planned with his surgery. In fact, major complications occurred that were life changing. 'They've taken my leg,' Jeff told us.

'What do you mean?' I asked.

'Yeah, they've taken it, it's gone,' Jeff said again.

Cyril and I looked at each other. We couldn't be hearing correctly. Surely he wasn't telling us that his leg had been amputated. 'So, they cut your leg off, is that what happened?' I asked.

'Yeah, that's right,' Jeff told us for the third time.

After we hung up the phone, we hugged each other and cried. How could this possibly happen to Jeff. We went to the Vo Rogue Plate the next day and afterwards we went to the hospital to see Jeff. His face was grey, and he looked terrible, but as our visit progressed Jeff picked up and the colour came back into his face. Jeff has always been the cup half full person, never the cup half empty.

'You are just so upbeat, Jeff,' I said to him. 'I think my bottom lip would be stapled to the floor if it were me.'

'Well that won't do you any good, Lynlea,' Jeff assured me. 'You can't look back, you can only look forward, and once my stub heals I will be fitted with a prosthetic leg. I'll be right then.' Such a remarkable attitude!

Jeff held a trainer's licence and at the time of his surgery he had Cymone's horse Fusi Fox in work. Daniel was riding him trackwork. 'The Fox' was sent to the paddock for a long spell while Jeff completed rehabilitation. Jeff did an awesome job accepting his prosthetic leg and with Cymone's help, Jeff was able to continue training once he got his health back on track. Jeff trained Fusi Fox to win three races, including one with Cyril on board at Warwick on 27 May 2017. Cyril was very happy to once again wear the famous brown jacket, white hooped sleeves and white cap to victory.

* * *

In early April 2018, my mother's health began to rapidly decline. Our kids were very close to their grandmother, and she just adored them all. I called Braidon and told him his grandmother was dying and it would be good if he, Amy and their daughter Erika could fly up to see her one more time. Erika, our first grandchild, was born on 25 October 2014 and of course she is absolutely fabulous, and my mother thought so too.

Braidon booked tickets for the family to fly up on 15 April straight after the races. He was riding Two Hats that day at Pakenham for Aaron Purcell in the MJ Bourke hurdle, a feature event. Two Hats was the $1.70 favourite for the race. Braidon won the JJ Houlahan Hurdle on Two Hats at Ballarat the previous season. Cyril and I were there that day. I've never been more excited on a racetrack and that's saying a lot. Cyril didn't say much at all, he was teary. We were very proud parents.

Things didn't go Braidon and Two Hats' way at Pakenham and they fell.

Braidon suffered a minor concussion and, in hindsight, shouldn't have flown, but the concussion didn't really hit him until the next day. Although she was very weak, my mother was delighted to see Braidon and his family walk into her room. Erika, who was only three and a half at the time, couldn't say 'great grandmother', she called my mother 'Gee Gee'. Erika sang to her Gee Gee which was just lovely. The family stayed for two days which went by quickly, and soon after, Braidon said goodbye to his grandmother for the last time. She passed away on 23 April 2018.

The following week, we flew to Warrnambool with Daniel to watch Braidon and Two Hats compete in the Galleywood Hurdle, a feature race of the Warrnambool Racing Carnival. Braidon was confident that the horse had taken no harm from his fall at Pakenham and even more confident that they would make amends for their error in the MJ Bourke and win the famous race, which they did.

As we clapped and cheered Braidon down the straight, past the winning post and back into the winner's circle, we could never have contemplated what fate had in store for our son less than 12 months later, and how Cyril and I would be faced with the most challenging time of our lives as parents.

* * *

Sunday 14 April 2019 started out well. Cyril and I had the typical chores to do with the horses first and foremost and then Jeff, Cymone and Daniel came out for lunch. Braidon was riding at Pakenham—which was the same meeting that he had fallen from Two Hats the year before. Cyril had a permit from the local fire warden to light four fires around the property. They were only small fires and conditions were good, so he was busy doing that as well.

Braidon's first ride for the day was on a horse called Startierra (also trained by Aaron Purcell). Braidon had won on him at his previous start in a maiden hurdle at Terang. As they came into the straight the first time, they fell at the jump. The fall looked to be a heavy one.

Braidon was slammed into the ground. The horse was uninjured, and got up, jumped every jump in the race and was first past the post. I was very worried about Braidon and immediately called Amy who was on track. Former star jumps jockey Shane Jackson ran up to where Braidon was and by now, Braidon was sitting in the ambulance and gave Shane the thumbs up. I asked Amy to ensure that Braidon didn't drive home. She promised me she would be the one driving and from all reports Braidon had injured his right knee, which he had injured before in a previous fall. The stewards in Victoria are awesome. They know how much I worry about Braidon and they had him call me when he returned to the saddling enclosure.

Later in the day, Cyril and I called Braidon to see how he was feeling. He was in the car on the four-hour journey home to Warrnambool. He was icing his knee and in good spirits. Amy was driving, with Erika asleep in the back seat. Daniel called Braidon a few hours after we called and apart from his knee, all was good.

Later that night I couldn't get to sleep. I forgot to close the windows to our bedroom when Cyril lit the fires and the smoke was lingering inside. Also, for the first time ever, I took my mobile phone into our bedroom. I had always previously turned it off at night time and turned it on again the next morning. However, the alarm clock beside the bed had broken so I took my phone to the bedroom to use it as my alarm.

At around 10.30pm I received a text from Amy. It read, 'I have just taken Braidon into the hospital his headache is getting worse I'll ring you if I need you.'

I replied, 'OK. I didn't realise he had hurt his head. Please keep me informed. Phone is by the bed. Thanks Amy.'

I told Cyril about the text. He wasn't overly concerned, and he soon fell asleep. I still couldn't sleep though so I went to Braidon's room to escape the smoke, but I didn't sleep a wink. Amy soon sent me photos of Braidon on a bed in the ED wearing a neck brace. The texts kept coming, then this: 'Things aren't looking good, I'll call you soon.'

I waited for her call but it didn't come. I tried to call her but she didn't pick up. Amy then sent this by text, 'Sorry lots of doctors coming and going, he has a bleed on the brain so they want to fly him to Melbourne ASAP.'

Oh my god. How could this be happening? I was nearly sick from worry about Braidon and so worried about Amy trying to deal with this on her own. I wanted to be there with Amy and Erika. Four months before, on 14 December 2018, Braidon and Amy had married in the most beautiful of settings in the Gold Coast Hinterland. Erika was their flower girl, Daniel a groomsman and Jess a bridesmaid. Everything was going so well for Braidon and for Amy. Fast forward a few months and Braidon was fighting for his life. I felt so helpless.

It was now 1.30am on Monday and I was completely distraught. I had already decided I was taking the first flight out of the Gold Coast to Melbourne and that was at 7.30am. I checked the flights and there were still five seats left on that plane. Cyril's alarm clock was set to go off at 3am. I didn't see the point in waking him before that time. There was nothing he could do. When Cyril got up, I started to tell him what was going on but I could barely get the words out of my mouth, I was crying so much.

Cyril told me he was coming to Melbourne with me, and we would have to quickly find a stable near the Turf Club for Dubai Gee Eye. I called Daniel soon after 3am. He didn't answer. I called him again and this time he did answer. I blurted out what had happened to Braidon.

'Calm down Mum,' Daniel told me. 'Braidon's fine. I spoke to him last night,' he said, trying to reassure me.

'No, he isn't,' I replied, and then explained to Daniel what was going on.

Daniel arranged a stable for the horse with trainer John Smerdon and Cyril gathered everything the horse would need and took him in. I booked one-way tickets to Melbourne and soon after 4am I was on the phone to Kevin Ring of the Australian Jockeys' Association (AJA) telling him what had happened. Kevin and the AJA do an extraordinary job in these situations, and I knew that Kevin and his colleagues would be able to provide the support and guidance we would need as a family to get through the nightmare that was unfolding.

At 5.30am the phone rang. It was the surgical coordinator from The Alfred. Amy had given him our phone number.

He began by telling me that Braidon had arrived safely and then commenced to explain to me Braidon's condition and the surgical procedure that he would have later that morning. I was completely overwhelmed, and I couldn't stop crying.

'I'm begging you, please save my son,' I pleaded to the stranger on the other end of the phone.

When we arrived at Tullamarine airport Des O'Keefe OAM, then Chairman of the AJA, was waiting to take us to The Alfred. Once at the hospital, we walked into the visitors lounge beside the Neurological Ward and Amy's face said it all. She looked like Cyril and I felt: completely devastated. Amy had arranged close friends to take care of Erika in Warrnambool until Amy's mother Janelle arrived from the Northern Rivers. Amy had made the long trip from Warrnambool to The Alfred by road on her own, not knowing what to expect once she got there. Her good friend Amy MacDonald made her way to the hospital to be with our Amy. Also there was CEO of the Victorian Jockeys' Association Matt Hyland and Lisa Stevens, one of Australia's pre-eminent sports psychologists who works with the VJA as well as the Western Bulldogs. Ron Hall from Racing Victoria also arrived. Their support was exceptional as was that of my close friend Dr Jillian Cavanagh, who was living and working in Melbourne at the time, and she arrived a few hours later.

While sitting around waiting for Braidon to get through his surgery, I suddenly became very anxious. I turned to Lisa and asked, 'Is there a chapel here?'

'Yes,' she replied, 'Would you like me to take you there?'

'Yes please,' I told her.

I felt compelled to make my way to God's house to tell him personally how precious Braidon is to me and to his whole family. I begged God not to take Braidon from us. Lisa and I sat in the chapel for about 20 minutes before we got a call to tell us that Braidon was out of surgery and that the surgeon was with the family.

The next 10 days were very difficult ones. Braidon came through the surgery well. So well in fact, that the day after his surgery, Braidon argued with the surgeon telling him that he was fine, and the surgeon needed to take the drain out of his head and discharge him. He told the surgeon that he was booked to do a television interview in the grandstand at Warrnambool racecourse later that week to promote the upcoming May Racing Carnival, and he had some good rides at the carnival that he had to take. The surgeon explained to Braidon that he had sustained a very serious injury and he was not out of the woods. There was only one place he was going to be anytime soon and that was in hospital.

Cyril went home the day after Braidon's surgery, he expected only improvement in the coming days. I stayed behind. I could not leave Braidon, and Amy appreciated the company each night. Amy and I spent between 12 and 14 hours each day at Braidon's bedside.

On the Wednesday morning, Jess called and I put Braidon on the phone to speak to her. They had a brief chat before I took the phone from Braidon and I soon hung up. Braidon and Jess always fought as kids, it was way beyond sibling rivalry, but now as adults they had a close bond. About 30 minutes later I received a text from Jess. It read, 'I'm having a bit of a meltdown at work. I don't know what to do. Think I'm feeling so overwhelmed because there is nothing I can do.' Jess included two crying emojis.

I stepped out of Braidon's room and called Jess. She was crying. Braidon's injury and the realisation of how close we came to losing him had hit her hard. I tried to reassure her the worst was over, but time would tell that wasn't anywhere close to the truth.

On the Wednesday night, Braidon's condition deteriorated. By the Thursday morning, Braidon had developed serious complications that required two MET calls. I kept Cyril always informed and on the Thursday night I called him in tears to tell him that our son was very, very sick, and Cyril needed to be with him, as well as with Amy and me. Cyril returned to Melbourne early the next morning. Daniel and Jess stayed in regular contact by phone, as did other family and friends.

We were blessed that Braidon was at The Alfred because the doctors and nursing staff there are world class and they pulled out all stops to get Braidon back on track. But it was a hard road.

While in hospital, Braidon developed expressive dysphasia, meaning that at times, particularly when he was tired, Braidon was unable to speak to us or even write down what he wanted to say. He understood everything being said to him but could not effectively communicate back. That's okay. Now I know why charades was created. Amy and I became very good at it and so did Braidon.

As he got stronger, the condition resolved itself but the pain in Braidon's head was at times excruciating, courtesy of that drain that was meant to be in his head for 24 to 36 hours, but stayed in for nine days. It was removed the day before he was discharged. Thank God for that. It was one less thing to worry about.

On Wednesday 24 April, Braidon was discharged from hospital. Cyril had returned to the Gold Coast by this time but asked that we all stay that night in Melbourne close to The Alfred just in case Braidon's condition deteriorated again. That was a very good suggestion because at 2.30am on ANZAC Day, Amy came into my room to tell me that Braidon was on the floor in the bathroom very sick. We took him straight to The Alfred ED and the doctors ran a number of high-level tests. The doctors were happy with the results and six hours later Braidon was feeling much better and was allowed to leave.

Those 10 days were an ordeal that none of us ever want to have to live through again. It was tough going but we got the result we prayed for. Lisa and Jillian kept Amy, Cyril and me upright throughout that time. I truly doubt we would have got through it without them.

On their way home to Warrnambool, Braidon and Amy dropped me to the airport and I flew back to the Gold Coast. Soon after, Braidon was reunited with Erika. He asked for her every day while he was in hospital.

A few days later, after tidying up some loose ends and packing a suitcase of fresh clothes, I flew back to Melbourne with Cyril and Daniel. We then drove to Warrnambool, where Cyril and Daniel stayed for a week, and I stayed for three.

Our family will be forever grateful to Amy, the staff at The Warrnambool Hospital, Air Ambulance Victoria and The Alfred

Hospital, whose collective efforts saved Braidon's life. We will always be most grateful to the Australian Jockeys' Association, the Victorian Jockeys' Association, and the Queensland Jockeys' Association, along with Racing Victoria, for the roles they played in supporting Braidon and all of us as a family.

One year after leaving The Alfred, Braidon and Amy walked into the Warrnambool Hospital for a very different reason. On ANZAC Day, 25 April 2020, Amy gave birth to our grandson Robbie Ray Small, our miracle boy.

CHAPTER 20

MUCH TO CELEBRATE

On 17 May 2019, the ultimate accolade was bestowed upon Vo Rogue. He was inducted into the Australian Racing Hall of Fame.

The event was held at Portside Wharf in Brisbane and I flew home from Melbourne for the event. With Braidon now on the mend, Cyril and I looked forward to enjoying the evening together with Jeff and Cymone.

As everyone was called to take their seats, I headed to the bathroom. When I came out, I found myself following a man into the function room. He walked straight over to where Cyril was sitting and he shook Cyril's hand. As he walked away towards his own table, I realised it was Hugh Bowman, who himself was being inducted into the Australian Racing Hall of Fame that night. I couldn't help but think, what a first-class act Hugh is and what a lovely gesture he made to Cyril.

Jeff and Cyril both went up on stage to accept Vo's Award as a new inductee. Brent Thompson and Pat Lalor were also being inducted into the Hall of Fame that evening, so they too were in attendance. Greg Radley was the MC and as usual, he was brilliant.

After Jeff accepted the award and was interviewed by Greg, telling him many stories about Vo, Cyril was called on to speak. Greg asked Cyril, 'How did you feel when you were out there all on your own, race after race, when they couldn't beat you no matter what they tried?'

Cyril replied, 'Yeah well, they did try a few different things. If it wasn't for two people in this room he would have won 28 races: Brent Thompson one, and Pat Lalor the other.'

The audience erupted with laughter and clapped appreciatively. Greg Radley responded, 'Well I know what Brent did, Brent rode Dandy Andy in that famous Australian Cup, goodness gracious me; what did Pat do?'

'Oh, Pat was commander and chief one day when we lost on protest,' Cyril replied.

Greg said, 'You lost on protest.'

'Yes,' Cyril confirmed.

Later, after discussing Vo, Greg said, 'And Vic Rail, we shouldn't go without giving him his due credit. Unorthodox to say the least.'

Cyril responded, 'He was a very good feeder, he was a very good mate of Jeff's, they were very good mates for a lot of years before Vo ever came along, they had a few arguments along the way. Yeah, he was a very good feeder and a good solid worker and the horse had the ability, we just reaped the rewards.'

Greg then said, 'If it were up to Vic, he [Vo] would have raced barefoot all his life.'

'I'm sure he would have,' Cyril agreed.

It was a great night and it was lovely to see Brent again. Cyril has bumped into Brent many times along life's journey. It is always wonderful to see them together as they hold such a unique place in Australian racing history. Once again though, it was sad that Vic wasn't alive to stand on the stage with Jeff and Cyril. Vic would have held court and been the star attraction on the night for sure.

Garry Roberts was quite upset that he did not receive an invitation to the event. I'm not sure why that was. Jeff and Cymone were invited by the Australian Racing Hall of Fame, while Cyril and I were invited by Racing Queensland that hosted the event that year.

Garry celebrates Vo's achievements each year with a lunch in the horse's honour. He has been doing that since 2014. Garry comperes the event and has as many as 100 people attend some years.

A doctor in the family

On 19 July 2019, I graduated with a Doctor of Philosophy (PhD) and became Dr Lynlea Small. It was one of the best days of my life for the sole reason that our family, including my brother Raoul, were all together. Only three months earlier my PhD held zero priority in my life, and the prospect of making the July graduation seemed a world away. Life takes many twists and turns that deliver good and bad outcomes. Our family has had our share of both, but that day wasn't just a good outcome, it was a great one, and there was so much more to celebrate than having a doctor in the family.

I haven't said anything about my brother previously because he played no part in Vo's story. But Raoul has played a huge part in our family life, never far away from any real action and has always been beyond supportive.

On the day of my graduation, I was, and still am, very proud of what I accomplished. In the two-year period from mid-2013 to mid-2015, I completed an honours degree and gained a Bachelor of Human Resource Management with First Class Honours while I worked full-time in a busy job and trained Dubai Gee Eye. My honours degree granted me entry to the Higher Degree Research program as a PhD candidate. I commenced my PhD in the areas of graduate employability in February 2016 and submitted it for examination in December 2018, one week before Braidon and Amy's wedding.

During that time, I continued to work full-time, while simultaneously training Dubai Gee Eye, and I had so many unexpected and traumatic things take place in my life. I was trampled by Millhousen in a simple paddock accident that left me with a fractured foot, sore ribs and pain in my abdomen. A close family friend suffered a life changing brain injury from a race fall, while another dear family friend was diagnosed with what would sadly turn out to be a terminal illness. And of course, as I already told you, my mother passed away. To top it off, my workplace that had for many, many years been a second home for me and a place of happiness, had become anything but. There were times when I was on my knees, and I could barely breathe.

Two months after I submitted my thesis, the examiners' reports were returned and the examiners required that I make some changes and complete additional work prior to being awarded my doctorate. I was completing that work at the time Braidon had his accident. Once Braidon's health improved, I focused fully on completing the work and I submitted my final thesis in June 2019.

I loved undertaking my PhD. Just on its own, undertaking my PhD was seriously a walk in the park. I often stayed behind after work in my office for three or so hours on weeknights to work on it, and I worked on it most weekends. Once I had collected all my data, I would spend up to 20 hours across Saturdays and Sundays analysing it, and writing up the results and the discussion—unless of course Dubai Gee Eye was racing, and I would work around his racing schedule.

Cyril always made sure I was well-fed, and he had coffee coming at regular intervals. He really is the best husband ever. My PhD started out as a labour of love for me. Once all the other variables that I was dealing with came into play, my PhD became an escape. For that I was thankful that I had something else to focus on.

Gold Coast Racing Hall of Fame Inductee – Cyril Small

While the family was proud of me, just one month later, Cyril would have us all brimming with pride. On 15 August 2019, Cyril was inducted into the Gold Coast Racing Hall of Fame. Once again, the whole family was there, but this time Jeff and Cymone joined us. It was a special night and Cyril so deserved the honour.

Cyril has been a marvellous contributor to the racing industry Australia-wide. Very few people can attest to working in the same job for 48 years, especially one as demanding, dangerous and competitive as the job of a professional jockey. Despite suffering numerous injuries, some of them life threatening or potentially career ending, Cyril has bounced back into the saddle and race ridden in every season of those 48 years to date. His goal is to reach the 50-year mark.

In his award acceptance speech, Cyril thanked the people in racing and he said, 'It [racing] has been my lifelong career, and it will be until the day I die.'

For some reason, when discussing Cyril and his riding of Vo Rogue, many members of the interstate press and now media tell a tale that suggests Cyril was plucked from the back blocks of country racing, parachuted into Flemington, Caulfield, Moonee Valley or Sandown, and then returned to the back blocks to resume his riding on the country tracks. Often, what was written about him and even discussed today in the press, was and still is quite fanciful.

For example, Trevor Grant, writing for the *Sunday Herald Sport* published on 15 October 1989, wrote:

> When the Queensland-based horse first came to prominence at the quality end of thoroughbred racing in Melbourne, Small had all the right credentials to support Andy Warhol's contention about the duration of fame in the lives of the mundane and mediocre. In fact, 15 minutes of glory might have seemed a bit much for a jockey who has only ever ridden one other horse to victory in open city company and has never been victorious on any other horse outside Queensland.

What an extraordinary thing to write! Those words are quite the contradiction to Peter Cameron's assessment in *The Courier Mail* on 10

March 1987 describing Cyril as, 'one of Brisbane's most accomplished money riders.'

Cyril has loved his life in the saddle and while he gets few race rides these days, he enjoys race riding as much today as he ever has. Cyril represents the very essence of what being a jockey is all about. He is hardworking, resilient, determined, always competitive but fair, and above all else, an exceptionally skilled horseman. He has never been a showman but always a professional and very humble. For Cyril, his life is defined by being a jockey. Riding racehorses is the only job he has ever had. Being a jockey is the only job he has ever wanted.

There is a popular saying that goes something like this: If you love what you do, you'll never work a day in your life. I think that saying was written for Cyril. He remains in the racing industry, in his words, 'because he can and because he wants to.'

* * *

In October 2020, Dave Weinert, President of the Gladstone Turf Club sent an SOS to Cyril to come up and ride. They didn't have enough jockeys to ride at their card and horses would have to be scratched because of that. Cyril was delighted to go up there and I went with him. We drove up and back and he got a winner, Liberty's Gift, for trainer Lee Kiernan, part-owned by Dave and his wife Judy.

Cyril had a great day out riding with the ladies who are all talented and very competitive. Racing in many country and provincial centres across Queensland just wouldn't happen without them, and their contribution to racing in that state is arguably more significant than that of the male riders. I use the terms females and males so you know who I am talking about. But the fact is, these ladies are jockeys—full stop.

A week following that trip to Gladstone, a friend of ours mentioned he was listening to John Laws' radio show and Cyril was being spoken about with praise for helping out the Turf Club. Cyril went back to Gladstone many weeks later but was out of luck. We still had a great time though. Dave sent out the SOS again in the Easter of 2022. Again, Cyril answered the call, he rode a winner, and we again had a great time.

Leaving a legacy

Across the years, we have met many people who tell Cyril that they followed Vo in their younger years and because of Vo and Cyril, they chose a career in the racing industry. What a wonderful legacy to leave a younger generation. Daniel and Braidon have inherited their father's deep love and passion for racing, and while they love nothing more than teasing their father, their love and respect for him runs deep.

In April 2020, Daniel moved to Warrnambool to be close to Braidon and later decided to try his hand as a jumps jockey too. He worked exceptionally hard and gained his licence in April 2022. He had his first ever race ride in a steeplechase. Not many jockeys in Australia can attest to that. He came fourth. Two weeks later, he rode at the Warrnambool Racing Carnival and finished third in a hurdle. Ten days after that, Daniel rode his first winner in a highweight on a horse called Ferago. Of course, the family was very proud.

Cyril has ridden at the same meeting as Braidon on several occasions over the years, but on 19 June 2022, he joined both Braidon and Daniel in the jockeys' room at a meeting at Warrnambool. The boys had several jumps rides between them, and Cyril had two on the flat. Cyril was just so excited to be there with his boys. It's moments like these and seeing the joy in Cyril's face as he stands beside his sons, all of them wearing their race riding attire, that reminds me why Cyril loves racing so much.

Warrnambool trainer Peter Lafferty told me that one morning soon after Daniel arrived, as the boys rode past him, he asked them, 'Which one of you is the better rider?'

He said they looked at each other and replied together, 'Dad is.'

Vo goes back to back in the 1990 Australian Cup at Flemington beating Better Loosen Up, Super Impose and Stylish Century. His connections rate this win the best of his illustrious career. *Photo: Martin King/Sportspix*

Top: When Vo wasn't being a superstar racehorse, he was giving our son Daniel pony rides. Vic, Vo, Daniel and Cyril, Hendra Spring 1990.
Photo: Lynlea Small
Bottom: Vic tried very hard to bring Vo back to full soundness after he suffered his injury at Kembla Grange in the Autumn of 1990. Here is Vic swimming Vo wearing his usual stable uniform of T-shirt, shorts and thongs, at Eagle Farm in the Spring of 1990. *Photo: Noel Pascoe*

Top: A highlight of Cyril's career was attending the iconic Birdsville meeting for Lynn Paton. The two had a lot of success together over the years. At Birdsville, they came away with a winner on each day (including Barrel A Fun) and numerous placings over the two day carnival. Barrel A Fun and Cyril, 6 September 2002.
Photo: John Snape

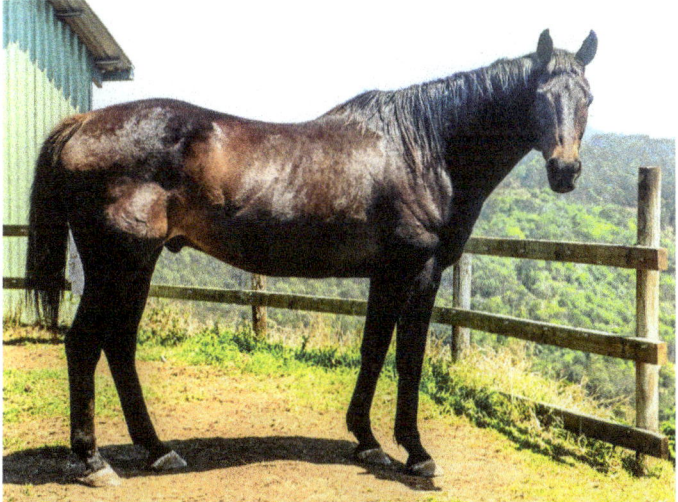

Middle: Vo and his favourite windsucking post. From here Vo had prize views across the Gold Coast skyline. 19 October 2002.
Photo: Lynlea Small

Bottom: Vo was inducted into the Queensland Racing Hall of Fame at the Sheraton Hotel in Brisbane on 23 August 2004. Jeff with former champion jockey Shane Scriven, Cyril and the legendary Darby McCarthy, who was also inducted that night.
Photo: Lynlea Small

Top: Daniel and Braidon were once Clerks of the Course at the Gold Coast Turf Club. They were ecstatic to ride back to scale with their father after Cyril won on Courtney's Wish for the late Ross Balcolmbe. Gold Coast 13 December 2008.
Photo: Trackside Photography
Middle: We were delighted to welcome John Tapp OAM and his crew to our home in March 2009 when they filmed a segment for Inside Racing. Daniel, John, me, Cyril and Jeff. 29 March 2009. *Photo: Lynlea Small*
Bottom: Our whole family will forever love Vo. This is one of my favourite photos. Braidon was born after Vo retired but he grew up with Vo and Vo was very much a part of his life. It isn't hard to see the deep love Braidon has for his Dad's champion. April 2009. *Photo: Lynlea Small*

Top left: Cyril and Zac Purton at Sha Tin racecourse 10 December 2015. Cyril and Zac have held the race riding record on the Northern Rivers of New South Wales collectively for 46 years. Cyril set the record with 55 wins in 1976 and held it until 2001. Zac has held it ever since with his record of 63 wins in the 2000/01 racing season. Zac is now considered one of the greatest jockeys in the world and lives in Hong Kong.
Top right: Cyril and Brent run into each other all over the place and it is always so lovely to see them together. They hold a unique place in Australian racing history. Here they are at Sha Tin on 13 December 2015.
Bottom: Cyril and Braidon caught up with Better Loosen Up at Living Legends on 24 January 2016. Vo and BLU had some stirring battles during their time on the racecourse and win, lose or draw, there was one thing for sure, both horses were champions. Sadly BLU crossed the rainbow bridge only a few months after this photo was taken.
Photos: Lynlea Small

Top: Vo achieved the ultimate accolade when he was inducted into the Australian Racing Hall of Fame in Brisbane on 17 May 2019. Cyril, Jeff, Cymone and I were privileged to be there on the night. *Photo: Lynlea Small*

Middle: On 15 August 2019 Cyril was inducted into Gold Coast Racing's Hall of Fame, a very fitting accolade and well deserved. Amy, me, Cyril, Daniel, Braidon and Jess. Aquis Park Gold Coast Turf Club. *Photo: Lynlea Small*

Bottom: Cyril had a great day riding at Gladstone against some of the talented ladies of racing. L-R: Trinity Bannon, Sonja Wiseman, Shannyn Stephan, Cyril, Natalea Summers, and Rebecca Wilson. 24 October 2020.
Photo: Gladstone Turf Club

Top: The May Racing Carnival at Warrnambool is one of the best carnivals anywhere. It was great to be there to see Daniel ride in his first carnival as a jumps jockey in 2022. He had a third which was exciting. Braidon rode for Lyn Shand. Her partner Jamie Bayliss is the son of the boys' mentor and close friend the late Bob Bayliss. L-R: Jamie Bayliss, Braidon, Cyril, Daniel, me, Patrick Ryan and Amy.
Bottom: In the past few years, Cyril and Jeff have reconnected with Peter Cook and they have a great time together lunching with Peter's long-time friends who include music legends Normie Rowe and Digger Revell. On 12 June 2022 we had a great night at the Rainbow Bay Surf Life Saving Club where we were privileged to watch Digger performed for the Cooly Rocks On Festival. L-R: Debby Osborne, Cyril, Normie Rowe, Jeff, Digger Revell and Peter Cook.
Photos: Lynlea Small

On 19 June 2022 Cyril realised one of his most joyous occasions as a jockey when he rode on the same card as Daniel and Braidon at Warrnambool. L-R: Me, Cyril, Daniel, Braidon, Robbie, Amy and Erika.
Photo: Amy Small

* * *

As I look back on the remarkable journeys and lives lived by a group of people and their extraordinary racehorse who are now a part of Australian racing folklore, it's not hard to get a little emotional. Sometimes it just seems so surreal.

The journey continues for Jeff and Cyril who today remain the very best of friends, a friendship (or bromance as they are now called), that has stood the test of time—close to 40 years. That is in itself something to celebrate. And of course, Debby and Jeff remain great friends and catch up when time permits. In more recent years, Jeff and Cyril have reconnected with Peter Cook and they regularly enjoy each other's company and that of some of Peter's long-time friends.

Jeff and Cymone attend our special family events, get-togethers, or they just drop in for a coffee. When we are out and about together, Cymone refers to us as the Perry-Smalls.

Jeff and Cymone were guests at Braidon and Amy's wedding, and Jeff was acknowledged in the speeches for the loyal support and friendship he has given all our family over many decades. After the speeches finished, Jeff found himself surrounded by the trainers and jockeys from Victoria who had attended, all wanting to talk to him about Vo and his racing career.

Regarding Jeff and Cyril's lengthy and close friendship, one trainer said to me, 'Wow, you just don't see that today, that loyalty in racing.'

I replied, 'No, you don't!'

Vic and Vo at Nudgee Beach at dawn, August 1987. Photo: Noel Pascoe

THE CHAMPS THAT WERE IN YEARS GONE PAST
LIKE PHAR LAP, FLIGHT AND RISING FAST
ALL RACED TO FAME BEFORE MY TIME
I DIDN'T SEE THEM IN THEIR PRIME.

THE YEARS SINCE THEN THAT I HAVE SEEN
OF RACING AND THE BEST THERE'S BEEN
I'VE SEEN THE CHAMPS ALL COME AND GO
BUT NEVER SEEN A HORSE LIKE VO.

YOU'D SAY IT'S RARE TO FIND A HORSE
TO LEAD AND WIN AT ANY COURSE
YOU'D HAVE TO SEARCH A THOUSAND MILE
TO FIND A HORSE SO VERSATILE.

HIS STRENGTH HAS SURELY HAD ITS TEST
WHEN CHALLENGED BY OUR NATION'S BEST
THEY'VE TRIED TO MATCH HIM FROM THE START
HE FIGHTS THEM OFF AND BREAKS THEIR HEART

TO DESCRIBE THE HORSE OR FIND A TERM
LIKE COURAGE, STRENGTH OR SPEED TO BURN
ALTHOUGH THESE WORDS CAN'T BE DENIED
I'D CALL HIM CLASS PERSONIFIED.

NO MATTER WHAT MAY BE ACHIEVED
IN RACES WON OR STAKES RECIEVED
HE IS THE GREATEST HORSE BY FAR
AND VO ROGUE YOU'RE A SUPERSTAR

Brilliant artist and friend Rick Sinclair sent Vo a congratulations card and included a poem he wrote for him after Vo won the 1989 Australian Cup.

ACKNOWLEDGEMENTS

I came upon a community Facebook platform that discussed Vo and his champion status. One post that stood out from all others read, 'The first words I ever spoke were *"Go Vo Go!"*'

I have been surprised that over the years no one has attempted to write about one of the greatest stories in Australian racing history, the story of Vo Rogue and that of his human friends. Much has been written about Vo and his connections but until now, each story has been told in isolation and they haven't always been factual.

I took it upon myself to change that, and in accomplishing what I set out to do, I have many people to thank for making this book a reality. They are old friends, and new ones who I have met in the past year or so, and each contribution was as enthusiastic as the next.

First and foremost, I would like to thank members of Team Vo: our very dear friend Jeff Perry, my wonderful husband Cyril Small, the woman behind Team Vo Debby Osborne, and Garry Roberts, whose collective contributions to the book are beyond significant. I would also like to thank Jeff Wilson, Ray Murrihy, Peter Cook, Brent Thompson, Michael Kerr, and Dr Lester Walters for sharing their stories and insights.

Thank you to my new friend Josh Rodder who not only filled in many statistical gaps from a Victorian racing perspective but provided new and important networks along the way. Thank you to Rod Fuller who provided statistical information about the Northern Rivers racing region, and to Racing Queensland's media team for their support.

Thank you to Des O'Keefe OAM and Dr Jillian Cavanagh for providing feedback on the manuscript from a reader's perspective. Thank you to John Harms for giving me some great pointers, and to Ben Dobson for the introduction to John. I also greatly appreciate the assistance from Gary Kliese, Wayne Gannon, Kerry Munce, Cindy Hurley, Natasha Wood, Peter Bredhauer, and Alison Raaymakers. And thank you to Father Joe Giacobbe who has the best modern day 'bush telegraph system' in the country, and to Greg Miles for his swift response.

To the professional photographers who have brought this book to life with their extraordinary photographic talents, thank you. They are Noel Pascoe, Colin L Bull, Steve Hart, Martin King, Bruno Cannatelli, Grant Peters and John Snape. A special thank you also to Mrs Glen Tandberg for allowing me to use work from the collection of her extraordinarily gifted husband and cartoonist, the late Ron Tandberg.

Thank you so very much to the highly professional and talented team at Melbourne Books. Working with this team has been an absolute pleasure and a seamless experience from start to finish for me. I would like to give a special mention to Mickayla Borthwick for her editing excellence. You have a stellar career ahead of you, my young friend.

Finally, I am indebted to John Tapp OAM who for decades and from afar I admired and greatly respected. I am deeply honoured that John has taken a keen interest in this book, has provided guidance and advice to me that was invaluable in getting to the final product, and afforded me the greatest privilege in writing the Foreword.

THE AUTHOR

Lynlea Small has been privileged to spend the majority of her life immersed in the thoroughbred racing industry as the wife of Cyril Small, a gentle man, a brilliant horseman, and the jockey of former champion racehorse Vo Rogue. Along the way she has gained a deep knowledge of racing, while she learned to train racehorses in her own right, support her two sons Daniel and Braidon to forge a career in jumps racing, and guide her daughter Jessica as she embarked on her career along a different pathway.

For the past 20 years, Lynlea has been equally immersed in the tertiary education sector where she works and has excelled academically with the highlight being awarded a Doctor of Philosophy (PhD) degree.

Lynlea had a front row seat throughout Vo Rogue's career. Her in-depth knowledge, coupled with her strong research skills and well-honed writing ability, have resulted in a book that perfectly captures the story of a cult hero who captivated a nation with feats that catapulted him and his connections into Australian racing folklore.

For Lynlea, this book represents her contribution to the history of horse racing in Australia.

On 19 July 2019 I graduated with a PhD. This is one of the greatest moments of my life for no other reason than we were all together having nearly lost Braidon to a race fall only three months earlier. My family is my greatest achievement. L-R: My brother Raoul Daniel, Amy, Braidon, Jess, Daniel, Erika, me and Cyril. *Photo: Lynlea Small*

The really magnificent spectacle in racing is the horse who goes to the front, dictates the pace to his or her own liking, and still endures. Real champions of the turf are few and far between. Champions who are front runners from any distance between 1200m and 2000m are as rare as a 1934 penny.

— Peter McFarline
The Age 17 February 1988

Other racing books published by Melbourne Books:
www.melbournebooks.com.au

Fields of Omagh
Kristen Manning

Manikato: 'The Man'
Adam Crettenden

Prince of Penzance:
Kristen Manning

Ride to Win
Greg Hall

Sport of Queens
Shane McNally

The Gauch
Kristen Manning

www.ingramcontent.com/pod-product-compliance
Lightning Source LLC
Chambersburg PA
CBHW040250170426
43191CB00018B/2366